W9-DDH-921

COPING
W I T H

Bias
Incidents

Barbara Moe

THE ROSEN PUBLISHING GROUP, INC./NEW YORK

Published in 1993 by The Rosen Publishing Group, Inc.
29 East 21st Street, New York, NY 10010

Copyright 1993 by Barbara Moe

First Edition

Library of Congress Cataloging-in-Publication Data

Moe, Barbara.
    Coping with bias incidents / Barbara Moe.
       p.   cm.
    Includes bibliographical references and index.
    Summary: Discusses bias acts based on prejudice, explaining why they are wrong and how to stop them.
    ISBN 0-8239-1606-5
    1. Prejudices—Juvenile literature. 2. Prejudices—Case studies—Juvenile literature. [1. Prejudices.] I. Title.
    BF575.P9M64 1993
    303.3'85—dc20   93-21721
                               CIP
                               AC

Manufactured in the United States of America

Contents

1	What Is Bias?	1
2	The Origins of Bias	24
3	Where Does Bias Occur?	46
4	Kinds of Bias	72
5	Handling Bias Incidents	86
6	Hope for the Future	127
	Appendix	144
	For Further Reading	146
	Index	149

ABOUT THE AUTHOR ◇

Barbara Moe has a Bachelor of Science degree in Nursing from the College of Nursing and Health, University of Cincinnati, and a Master of Science degree in Nursing from Ohio State University. She received her Master of Social Work degree, as well as a certificate in Marriage and Family Therapy, from the University of Denver.

Author's Note: All of the anecdotes in *Coping with Bias Incidents* are true. Some come directly from those affected by bias. Others come from newspaper and magazine accounts. Most of those telling their stories are high school students who took the time to respond to a questionnaire and participate in interviews. Only their names and certain circumstances have been changed.

CHAPTER 1

What Is Bias?

Charity, sixteen

Charity does volunteer work at a children's hospital, participates in her church youth group, baby-sits, and is a cheerleader. She remembers a wonderful summer vacation with her family when she was thirteen. The trip had only one bad moment. The family had stopped at a motel with a prominently displayed "vacancy" sign. When her dad went in to get a room, the young man on duty shook his head. "Sorry," he said. For a moment Charity's dad was too upset to drive on. They parked under an oak tree and watched as a white family drove in. As Charity's dad had predicted, *that* father walked out of the office with a key in his hand. Charity remembers feeling "shocked, angry, frustrated, and furious." She adds: "Some people are ignorant. Their loss."

This is a classic example of racial prejudice. Believe it or not, Charity's story is true. Similar bias incidents happen every day in small towns and big cities throughout America.

Jacob, fourteen

"I had just moved to a new school. In art class one day, some kids asked me what hospital I was born in. I said, 'Jewish Hospital.' They said, 'Aren't you Christian?' I answered, 'No, Jewish.' After that, they started calling me 'Foolish Jewish' and 'Jacob Jewish,' and other names like that. At first I made faces at them and fought back. (I came from a tough neighborhood, so I knew how to fight.) A couple of years later, though, I decided to start ignoring their meanness and began treating them nicely. This confused them. It was sort of funny. I don't think they even remembered *why* they hated me. They just knew they did."

Jacob's story shows anti-Semitism and the irrationality of prejudice.

Anna, seventeen

"I was sitting around with some friends, and we were talking about dating. I'd been friends with this guy Jack for a long time. He looked right at me and said, 'I would never date a blonde; I hate blonde women. They're so dumb.' Then he laughed. I ignored him, but later when we were alone I confronted him. He said he was only joking. (Yeah, right!) I felt worthless and betrayed. Every time I think back to that incident, I feel awful."

Just a joke? Perhaps to Jack, but not to Anna. Her story illustrates sexism.

Bill and Stan, sixteen

> Bill and Stan walked into an upscale computer store because Bill's father had asked them for their opinions on some equipment. (The boys knew much more about computers than Bill's dad.) Bill and Stan couldn't find anyone to help them; the clerks ignored them. The salespeople all assumed that because these two young men were high school students, they didn't have money to spend.

Bill and Stan experienced age bias because they were young. Often, however, older people also suffer from age bias. An employer decided that Cal, a man of sixty, was too old to work even though Cal had excellent productivity and enjoyed superb health.

Anita, eighteen

> Anita does not flaunt her lesbianism, but word gets around. Especially the word that a classmate is gay.

> Last June Anita, an all-state soccer player, graduated from high school with honors. When she picked up her diploma at the graduation ceremonies, someone in the audience called out, "Dyke!" Says Anita, "My grandparents heard that, and it hurt—not only them but me."

Anita's story illustrates bias against homosexuals. Because of this bias, students who are gay are at high risk for dropping out of school, for drug and alcohol abuse, and even for suicide.

BIAS INCIDENTS

What do all of the examples above have in common? They are all bias incidents.

What is a bias incident? A bias incident is any action a person commits against another person because of having a prejudice or making a prejudgment based on race or ethnicity, sex, religion, age, occupation, social class, sexual orientation, or any number of other categories.

Why do we worry about bias incidents? Because they are hurtful, for one thing. Because they are dangerous, for another thing. Probably no one reading these words has not heard of the Rodney King case. This black man's beating by white Los Angeles police officers and the subsequent acquittal of the policemen touched off riots that left fifty-eight people dead, many injured, and huge losses in property damage.

Unless we learn to live in peace, we will see many more bias incidents. Some will cause soul-wounding; others will cause death. After the riots, Rodney King made a plea for harmony in which he asked: "Can we all get along?" To which he answered: "Let's try to work it out."

ARE WE ALL ALIKE? OF COURSE NOT!

The United States is a country of diversity. Diversity can be a positive force, making life more interesting for all of us. But differences can lead to conflict.

Cultural diversity is one kind of difference. According to Congressman George Miller in the book *Children of Color*, "Minority group members—Blacks, Hispanics, American Indians, and Asians—constitute 4 percent of all adults in the country and 20 percent of children under seventeen. By the year 2000, it is projected that one third of all school-age children will fall into this category." We must learn to get along.

Consider the following news items:

- A Hispanic coalition in Albuquerque, New Mexico, considered boycotting a hair salon chain after a manager sent a memo ordering employees to speak only English.
- The U.S. Commission on Civil Rights recently urged political leaders to stop "Japan-bashing." The Commission added, "Political leaders contribute to the problem when they unthinkingly lash out at Japan as the cause of United States economic difficulties."
- A black bus driver attacked with racial slurs and death threats by three "skinheads" was awarded $1.75 million in damages by a Chicago jury.
- The United States Surgeon General called the brand name and the product Crazy Horse Malt Liquor "an insult to Indians." The governor of South Dakota agreed. "It is disheartening that they have chosen to associate a malt liquor with the proud Native American culture." (Crazy Horse, a respected Sioux warrior, died in 1877.)

The above are examples of bias incidents—racial, ethnic, and cultural—reported by the press. Although these terms have somewhat different meanings, distinctions have blurred over the years. As we have seen, people can hate and put others down because of many characteristics. These include gender, sexual orientation, religion, social class, or any number of other biases.

Gordon Allport, author of *The Nature of Prejudice*, says that for most purposes the term "ethnic" is preferable to "race." Neither term, however, covers all the categories of people who are the frequent targets of bias incidents.

HATE CRIMES INCREASE

Hate groups in the United States have grown to a record number, according to Joseph T. Roy, chief investigator for Klanwatch, a monitoring group based in Montgomery, Alabama. From 1990 to 1991, the number of hate groups rose by 27 percent. Ku Klux Klan groups increased from 69 to 97, and neo-Nazi groups increased from 160 to 203. New York City reports that between 1986 and 1990 hate crimes increased by 80 percent; 70 percent of those arrested were under the age of nineteen. In 1989–1990, according to a survey by the *Boston Globe*, hate crimes increased by 41 percent in Los Angeles and by 33 percent in Boston.

Roy says that hate groups are refining their message. Instead of talking hatred of minority groups, they stress love of whites. They try to sound as if they have the answers to the problems of society. Unfortunately, Roy observes, they don't. He believes the current mood of the country is frightening because hate groups want to blame all the problems of society on a particular target.

A Civil Rights Commission report, *Civil Rights Issues Facing Asian Americans in the 1990s*, says, "Racial tension appears to be escalating across the country, yet political leaders have done little to defuse it. The general absence of moral leadership carries over to the civil rights concerns of Asian Americans."

Hate crimes against another group, homosexuals, have also risen. Nationally in 1991, violence against gays increased by 31 percent. According to the National Gay and Lesbian Task Force Policy Institute, 1,822 incidents of violence were reported in five major cities in 1991, as opposed to 1,389 in the same cities in 1990. A federal law passed in 1990, the Hate Crimes Statistics Act, requires the Attorney General to begin collecting data on hate crimes.

Author James Lee Burke, quoted in *The Bloomsbury Review* (June 1992), says: "If I have a concern about the times in which we live, it's that there are so many people in this country who will not accept the fact that we are a pluralistic nation. These organized hate groups—the Moral Majority, the Klan, the extreme right wing, and even some groups who are extreme on the left side of the equation—they all have the same emotional common denominator. They're not necessarily all bad people, but many of them are. They just can't accept that in a pluralistic society we all have to learn to live with each other. And that a gay person, or a Black or Oriental person, a Mexican immigrant, or an elderly person all have the same rights, under the Consitution and in the eyes of God, as everyone else. People who can't accept that consume themselves with their fears and anxieties. They live in vitriol. They boil in their own juices. And these demagogues we have in our midst have one message only: 'Blame your fellow man for your problems.' And it's well received because there are so many people willing to believe the source of their discontent is not in themselves but is in someone else."

WHO COMMITS HATE CRIMES?

Hate crimes can be committed by any person or group against another person or group. Here are some examples.

- Four young white men attacked a fourteen-year-old black teenager and his sister while the two were walking home from school in the borough of the Bronx, New York. The attackers stole three dollars from the young girl and began cutting her hair. They then sprayed the two with white shoe polish, saying, "Y'all are going to be white today."
- In New York City that same week, police reported that ten to fifteen black teenagers boarded a city bus, punched and kicked a seventeen-year-old white girl, and got off the bus.
- In Chicago, six black children were charged with hate crimes after they allegedly set a pit bull on an eight-year-old white girl and her six-year-old mentally disabled sister.
- In Denver, Colorado, Judy Guillory, who is African-American and an employee of the Coors Brewing Company, was driving back to work after lunch. She tried to ignore three teenagers in another car who shouted racial slurs at her. One of the young men climbed through the sun roof and directed a Hitler salute at Guillory. Her companion wrote down the teenagers' license plate number, and the two women called police. The teenagers, reportedly skinheads, face charges of ethnic intimidation. If convicted, they could be sentenced to two years in a juvenile correctional center.
- In New York City, a car driven by a Hasidic Jew jumped the curb and killed a black child. In the violence that followed, a young Jewish man was killed, and a black man was arrested for the murder.

Elie Wiesel, winner of a Nobel Peace Prize, lost most
of his family members in Nazi death camps when he was
only fifteen. Wiesel, now a citizen of the United States,
believes that *fanaticism* is responsible for hate crimes,
which are on the rise not only in the United States but all
over the world. What is fanaticism? Fanaticism is an all-encompassing
word whose meanings include racism, bigotry, and ethnic
hatred. Speaking to 1992 graduates and quoted in *PARADE*
magazine (May 24, 1992), Wiesel echoes the words of
Rodney King: "Can't all our citizens—white Americans
and African-Americans, Hispanics and Asians, Jews and
Christians, Jews and Moslems, young and old—live
together and work together and face together their
common challenges?"

Let's try to understand the meaning of some powerful
words by attaching them to people.

PREJUDICE

Priscilla

Priscilla sits in an ice cream parlor in Iowa with her
boyfriend. "I don't like blacks or Jews," she says.
"Blacks are loud and angry; Jews are aggressive and
stingy." Priscilla lives in a town of five hundred
people. Not one black person or Jewish person lives
in her town. She is prejudging with no basis in fact.
Although prejudice can be positive, it usually is not.
Prejudiced views of various groups are characterized
by preconceived opinions, judgments, and feelings
that lack substance.

Even if Priscilla had met blacks or Jews, she could not realistically hate an entire category of people. Every person is different. Priscilla is not only showing prejudice; she is also stereotyping.

STEREOTYPES

Steven

Most people consider Steven a likable guy. He speaks deliberately, as if he has thought about what he's preparing to say. Steven has credibility; people tend to believe him. His friends, however, have heard him say: "Let's not go to Las Delicias; it's always full of Mexicans." Or, "Everyone who goes to that school is a gang member." Or, "The people on that side of town don't care what their neighborhood looks like."

Steven is using stereotypes. A stereotype is a specialized and oversimplified idea about a person or a group of people.

Nancy, fifteen

"When I was twelve, our family went skiing for a week. On the second morning the lift malfunctioned, and a bunch of people (myself included) found themselves suspended in midair. A guy in the chair ahead of me turned around and pointed at me. "That girl has red hair," he said. "Pretty soon she's going to lose her temper for all of us."

Nancy felt as if her face had caught fire. The remark was her first experience with stereotyping, and she didn't like it.

Alicia, fourteen

"Because I listen to heavy metal music and have guy friends who wear their hair long, people think I smoke, use drugs, and am generally all mixed up. The stereotypes really upset me."

Foster, sixteen

"Another black kid and I were going to summer school at Waterside Country Day. The school is in a wealthy white suburb at the end of the bus line. On the first day we got off the bus and started walking toward school. This police car cruised up, and an officer jumped out. 'What are you guys up to?' he snarled. 'Going to school,' I said. 'Sure,' he said. The police officers made us get in their car. They drove us to the school office and marched us in there like we were criminals. But the secretary had our names on a list. The cops left, and the secretary apologized for them. I felt furious and humiliated."

Armando, seventeen

"You hear stereotypes all the time. If you grew up in a Hispanic family or came from a different economic background, you weren't expected to make it."

Lan, eighteen

"Sometimes they clump you together with others who are supposedly just like you. Asians are all scientists, for example. That is not true, but you feel the pressure."

DISCRIMINATION

Donald

Donald was taking care of the desk at his family's motel in Kansas when Charity's father walked in and asked for a room. Donald carried his preconceived notions about black people a step beyond prejudice to discrimination.

Discrimination is unjustifiable negative behavior directed at a racial or other group, or members of such a group. Prejudice is often at the root of discrimination.

RACISM

"Racism," says Catherine Meeks, Ph.D., "is a combination of prejudice and power." A person can be prejudiced without having power, but whites have power in our society because they have accepted a legacy of power left to them by their ancestors.

Dr. Charles King, founder of the Urban Crisis Center in Atlanta, Georgia, points out that racism is much more than prejudice. Racism is so inbred in our society that it adversely affects all minority people. According to King, the system and its benefits are structured for the white majority.

Ronald

Ronald, a Caucasian, is in charge of hiring at an agency that places workers in temporary jobs. While in college, Ron was a member of a white fraternity. Former members (alumni) often come in to apply for jobs through Ronald's agency. Ron would be shocked to hear anyone imply that he is a racist. He does not mean to prejudge and discriminate. Anglo men hear about the available jobs through an informal network. Although no one means any harm, this is a racist situation. Racism is based on the false premise that people of one race are superior to those of another race.

In *Reducing Adolescent Prejudice*, Nina Gabelko and John Michaelis define institutional racism (as in the above example) as "deeply embedded patterns of discrimination in economic, labor, legal, educational, and many other institutions against less powerful racial groups." This is one of the many forms of racism.

Racist remarks, such as Polish jokes, are another form of racism. The people who tell such jokes and those who laugh at them often mean no harm. They're just "having fun." Fun at someone else's expense. Each stage of prejudice, if not stopped, can lead to a more violent form of discrimination, such as cross burning or lynching. Racism prevents the development of self-esteem and keeps people of color from obtaining adequate health care, education, and jobs.

BIGOTRY

Bertram

Bert pushes literature about his religious beliefs into the hands of others, whether or not they want it. He believes that his way is the only way. One evening he met Naomi, sixteen, at a rock concert. He stood in front of her so she could not pass and forced her to listen to his speech. Naomi told Bert she wasn't interested; she already had her religion. "What is it?" asked Bert. "I'm Jewish," said Naomi. At this point, Bert turned almost purple and told Naomi she was the anti-Christ. Naomi managed to sputter a few words, then realized that nothing she said would change the mind of this bigot. She walked away feeling "angry and disenchanted with humanity."

Bigots stubbornly hold on to *their* ways, beliefs, and opinions in spite of evidence to the contrary. Bigots do not bother listening to or considering the views of others. Their minds are closed.

STEREOTYPING, BIAS, BIGOTRY, AND RACISM

Terry Cross of the Northwest Indian Child Welfare Association, Portland, Oregon, tells a story to illustrate the meaning of some of these words. Two men meet for the first time. The Anglo-American greets the Native American with a firm handshake and a straight-on, no-nonsense look. He thinks this way of greeting shows respect. The Native American man's elders taught *him* to show respect with an averted gaze and a limp handshake. These two men greet each other in their cultural ways. When they part, the Native American mumbles, "Aggressive white man!" Meanwhile, his Anglo acquaintance is saying, "Passive Indian!"

Add bias and/or prejudice:

Anglo: "Indians are so passive. No wonder they can't find jobs."

Native American: "Whites are so aggressive. No wonder they take jobs away from the people who deserve them."

Now add bigotry:

Either man: "I hate those people!" (of whatever group)

Add a power differential, and you have racism:

Either man: "I hate those people, and I'm not going to let them have a job in my company."

Prejudiced *beliefs* may lead us to accept "facts" that are not true at all. Have you believed some of the following myths?

MYTHS AND FACTS

Myth: Those who commit bias crimes are usually thirty years of age and older.

Fact: Teenagers cause the majority of bias incidents. According to Pearl Gaskin in *Scholastic Choices*, in New York City in 1989, 62 percent of those arrested for bias incidents were under nineteen years of age.

Myth: Most bias incidents are committed by members of organized hate groups, such as skinheads.

Fact: Most bias incidents are committed by unaffiliated persons.

Myth: Young people born after the 1960s are more open toward those of other races than their parents were.

Fact: A recent survey by People for the American Way showed that racial attitudes of American young people are as divided as ever. Sixty-eight percent of blacks believed they suffered from discrimination; 52 percent of Hispanics and 49 percent of whites felt discriminated against. Sixty-five percent of all those surveyed *opposed* special employment opportunities for minorities, while 60 percent of blacks *favored* such programs.

Myth: If blacks receive higher education (four years of college), their salaries are the same as whites.

Fact: Blacks with four years of college earn $79.80 for each $100 whites earn. Black men with college educations earn only a few dollars more than white men who completed only high school. In July 1988, the unemployment rate for blacks aged sixteen to nineteen was 31.1 percent, twice the rate for white teenagers.

Myth: Black single mothers are all on welfare.

Fact: Only half of all black single mothers are on welfare.

Myth: Single mothers have kids so they can get welfare money and not have to work.

Fact: The national average cash allowance for families receiving Aid to Dependent Children is less than $5,000 per year.

Myth: Young black males are more likely to use drugs and alcohol than other youths— certainly more likely than white kids.

Fact: According to former Health and Human Services Secretary Louis Sullivan, white male students are twice as likely as their black counterparts to have tried cocaine.

Myth: Black young people are more likely to drop out of high school than white kids.

Fact: Figures for 1989, the most recent available, show that 93.7 percent of all black sixteen-

and seventeen-year-olds were enrolled in school, compared to 92.3 percent of whites in the same age group.

Myth: Having a chronic illness is the most life-threatening condition a young person can experience.

Fact: Statistics from around the world show that being female is one of life's most threatening conditions. Another life-threatening condition in the United States is to be a young black male.

Females: A study by the World Health Organization reveals that when food is scarce, girl children are fed less, breast-fed for a shorter time, and taken to doctors less often. For women of childbearing age, the denial of reproductive control can lead to death from illegal abortions.

Young black males: In his series *Countering the Conspiracy to Destroy Black Boys*, Jawanza Kunjufu presents the following statistics: In 1990 African-Americans made up 47 percent of the U.S. prison population. Because no scientific data show blacks as a violent group, we must conclude that bias is at least in part responsible for these numbers. According to Jewelle Gibbs in *Children of Color*, between 1960 and 1984 the suicide rate for black males between ages fifteen and twenty-four nearly tripled, from 4.1 to 11.2 per 100,000. Studies project that if the current rates continue, 70 percent of all African-American males will be unavailable to African-American women by the year 2000.

Many will be either dead, in jail, on drugs, unemployed, or mentally ill.

THE AMERICAN OBSESSION

Racial bias is only one category of prejudice, but it is a one that bears closer examination. In Studs Terkel's book *Race: How Blacks and Whites Think and Feel About the American Obsession*, Gilbert Gordon, an eighty-year-old white lawyer, says that all Americans carry with them the consciousness of race.

We could broaden that statement to say that tensions between groups, prejudices, and biases threaten to overwhelm us. Bias can tear us apart. The following stories from high school students indicate the range of bias incidents.

Jessica, seventeen

"Here's an example of things that go on in our school. I'm black and in an accelerated program. There are nine other blacks in the freshman class. We get the cold shoulder from the counselors and from the other students. They look at us as if they think we're stupid. One girl said to her friends: 'Be quiet, guys. We don't want to be like them; you know, blacks are loud.' I think it's pure ignorance. These people and their parents need to realize we all have to change for things to work out."

Elaine, fifteen

"I'm white. I was hanging out with a guy friend of mine who happens to be black. The black girls got hostile and acted prejudiced toward me, maybe because they were jealous. I sat down at the lunch table with these girls, and one of them said, 'No white girl should be sitting at this table, especially if she's a freshman.'"

Joe, sixteen

"I walked into this store in the suburbs with a white friend to buy some candy. As I stepped up to the counter, the saleslady said to me, 'Get that candy out of your pocket!' To her amazement, I was holding the candy in my hand. I put it on the counter and walked out."

In Terkel's book, Douglas Massey, professor of sociology at the University of Chicago, says, "Among black people there is frustration, anger, hatred. Among whites there is fear, hatred, denial . . . When you create two societies, so separate, so unequal, people at the bottom half are ultimately going to lash out at the people at the top half. There will be violence."

Cameron, seventeen

"We were in a recreation center in the inner city. I was on our school's ninth grade basketball team. We could hear loud whispers from the other team, 'There's the rich boys. They don't have any black kids on their team, except for one who acts white.' We kept our mouths shut about the calls; otherwise the ref would say, 'Rich kids whine.' I felt ganged up on and wanted to tell them off even though they outnumbered me. I felt helpless, so I didn't do anything but cuss under my breath. I didn't want to stoop to their level, but I became prejudiced to offset their hatred toward me."

Aaron, seventeen

"In ninth grade I was on the school bus on my way home when I heard derogatory comments about Jews coming from one kid. I paused for a minute. Then, using expletives, I started sternly telling the kid to shut up. I only knew how to fight his fire with my own fire of hatred toward bigots. As long as one person's hate ignites another's, bias will never end."

A person does not have to be a genius to understand Leah's opinion that prejudice is everywhere; one need only look around.

Leah, fifteen

"I go to a snobby high school. Most of the kids here are rich, well dressed, and preppy. My mom doesn't make a lot of money, and I like to dress really different. I shop at thrift stores and listen to different music. On my first day of high school, some snobbish, preppy girls made sarcastic, rude comments about my clothes."

Although Leah's perceptions probably have some validity, she seems to have some prejudices of her own.

LITTLE BOXES AND BIG BOXES

Has anyone ever gasped at the sight of your messy room? The cause of the problem may be too much junk that needs to be sorted into various categories. Get some cartons. Put all of last year's school stuff in one carton, old letters in another, and so on. Suddenly, you may be able to see through the mess.

We can do the same process of sorting in our minds. Thinking in categories (making generalizations) does not necessarily mean we are prejudiced. Gordon Allport says that certain "prejudgments" are necessary for daily living. We need to sort out the different ideas in our minds. For example, if clouds are gathering, we might decide to wear a raincoat. If we're going out to lunch and the restaurant is usually crowded at noon, we might decide to go at 11:30 a.m. instead. Based on our experiences of the past, we take certain actions.

A problem arises when we are lazy and use categories as an excuse for thinking. Allport says, "It costs the Anglo employer less effort to guide his daily behavior by the generalization, 'Mexicans are lazy,' than to individuate his workmen and learn the real reason for their conduct." Prejudgment turns into prejudice if these judgments do not change in the light of new knowledge.

As reasonable human beings, we have to walk a fine line. We must value ourselves and our identity (so that we can value others), but we must be careful not to get a "superiority complex."

PERSONAL IDENTITY: WHO AM I?

No matter who we are, we need to think well of ourselves. A good self-image (high self-esteem) is probably the most important characteristic any person can have. One way we find out who we are is to observe the ways in which we are similar to (or different from) others. This observation is a natural process of sorting out and categorizing. For example, if I have short chunky fingers and you have long slender fingers, does that mean my fingers are better than yours? If my skin is brown and yours is white, does that mean you are better than I am?

Researchers Darlene and Derek Hopson point out that people of color often see themselves as having low self-worth. In 1985 the Hopsons replicated a famous experiment that was first done in the late 1930s and early 1940s. In that experiment, Drs. Kenneth and Maie Clark reported that 67 percent of black children chose a white doll over a black doll. When the Hopsons repeated the experiment twenty-five years later, they found that 65 percent of black children still picked white dolls.

The Hopsons then undertook to change the black children's view of the dolls (and of the children themselves). The Hopsons, both black, consistently chose the black dolls in front of the children, they spoke positively about the black dolls, and they read stories depicting black children in positive ways. When they repeated the experiment a second time, 68 percent of the black children chose *black* dolls. The Hopsons concluded that one of the secrets of high self-esteem for black children is positive talk—positive role modeling and reinforcement of the goodness of their black identity.

WHO'S HURTING?

Prejudice hurts those who experience it, but bias also hurts those who harbor it. In many cases, those with a high degree of prejudice boost their shaky self-esteem by putting others down. Thinking they are special because they are of a certain race, ethnicity, gender, or religion gives them a false sense of reality.

On a scale of one to ten, how do you rate the level of self-esteem in the students and parents in the following story?

Officials at a suburban high school barred eight seniors from graduation ceremonies after a "prank" degenerated into sexist and racist graffiti and vandalism. The incidents left the school with a torn roof, human excrement at the main entrance, and defamatory graffiti against teachers and fellow students on the school walls.

One item of graffiti made obscene remarks about a female teacher. Another, written on the door of a Colombian-American teacher's room, said, "Mexican, go home. We don't want you here."

Parents of the students involved said the punishment was too severe. They argued that other seniors involved in graffiti incidents that year were being allowed to attend commencement exercises. The father of one of the boys said that he and other parents were organizing a petition drive to protest the discipline and perhaps would ask for the principal's removal.

What do you think? Letters and public opinion supported the principal and the consequences he imposed. In the next chapter we discuss some of the places where prejudice originates.

CHAPTER 2

The Origins of Bias

Jean, seventeen

As president of the International Club at her high school, Jean, an Anglo-American, attended a national conference on cultural diversity. For the first time in her life, Jean heard that racism in the United States is a "white problem." Anglo-Americans, said the speakers, must begin to take some of the responsibility for solving the problems of racism in our society.

Jean learned that white institutions perpetuate racism, and she didn't like what she heard. She herself had always been careful to be tolerant of others' differences. (Although some people may scoff, being respectful of the differences of others is a small step in the right direction. Some say that positive attitudes, although helpful, are not enough to make a difference.)

At the conference Jean seriously considered the impact of slavery, not only on blacks but on everyone. She learned that Jews have experienced similar intergenerational pain as a result of the Holocaust, a "megatragedy" that claimed the lives of six million Jews. Likewise, Native Americans have suffered from low self-esteem, lost opportunities, and extermination at the hands of their Anglo "conquerors."

Jean left the conference feeling exhausted. When she got back to school, she wanted to tell her classmates what she had learned. Most of them didn't want to hear. Here are two of their responses.

Ashley, fifteen

"In middle school, as a Mormon and as a white person, I became aware that the blacks and the Hispanics ran the school. Why not? They made up three fourths of the student population. If you weren't part of their clique, good luck. Whoever happens to be in power will never give it up."

Arthur, sixteen

"We have to solve the problem of racism? Are you kidding? Give me a break! Bias incidents happen to me every day because I'm black. I defend myself and my views. But the problem will never be resolved."

Some students of sociology contend that the blame is totally on the whites. They argue that the Caucasian race has despoiled the planet and is incapable of changing their ways to bring about a peaceful earth.

Most people contest that attitude and suggest that its proponents are themselves stereotyping whites. Here are the opinions of a few who hold the latter attitude.

Sally, eighteen

"As a white person who tries to overcome my own biases, I find myself getting a bit defensive when whites as a group are blamed for being prejudiced. Although I don't argue with the concept of white racism, my emotions get in the way. I know other Anglos must have similar reactions. Many whites would never say or do biased things to other people and therefore can't relate to those who do. When these people feel defensive and threatened, they may eventually be even less open to change. When they are blamed for the biases of others, they feel bad."

According to Sally, some people are either complacent or defensive because they can't believe one human being would treat another with such disrespect. And yet, haven't we all heard of such examples?

Gayle, fifteen

"My dad owns two apartment buildings. I heard him talk about the renters, and I said to him, 'Dad, you're prejudiced.' He said to me, 'Yes, I am. Blacks are a violent people.' Can you believe this? My mother (his wife) is originally from Mexico and I, therefore, am part Hispanic. His own wife and daughter are minorities. I can't believe him. His whole attitude blows me away!"

Howie, seventeen

"I'd like to know what you think the world would be like if Anglos totally 'gave up' and let people of color rule the world. Do you think the 'minorities' then holding the reins would be any more charitable than the whites are now?"

In an article entitled "America's Original Sin: The Legacy of White Racism," Jim Wallis writes that racism has to do with the power to dominate and enforce oppression. In the United States that power lies with whites. Wallis adds that although we see evidence of black racial prejudice against whites, these instances are usually in reaction to white racism. There is no such thing as "black racism," says Wallis, because blacks do not have the power.

How can we solve the problem of white racism? No one knows for sure. Wallis suggests that whites must first admit this reality: Theirs is a racist society. Second, the black community will have to devise strategies for overcoming white racism. Third, whites will have to help. (Others say that only whites can solve the problem because they have the power.) If whites would put pressure for change on economic, political, and social leaders, perhaps racism would eventually disappear. Others predict that the struggle will last forever.

Steve Charleston, a Native American, suggests that the wisdom to overthrow Western racism should come from his people. The year 1992 marked five hundred years of oppression of Native Americans. Charleston calls their fate in the United States "the American Holocaust."

Let's go back to Ashley and Arthur. They didn't want to hear what Jean had learned at the conference. Bias had touched their lives, and they had given in to it. They had closed their minds. We will return to Jean in Chapter 6. Meanwhile let's see if we can learn something about the origins of bias.

WHERE DOES BIAS COME FROM?

"No single theory of prejudice is adequate," says Gordon Allport. Nevertheless, if we are to try to figure out where bias comes from, we must consider some of the theories.

The Family Connection

The first and most common place where we are exposed to prejudice is in our families. In other words, if in our homes we hear black people called "niggers," whites called "honkies," or Hispanics called "spics," we are growing up with prejudice and negative stereotyping.

In Chapter 1 we had a brief introduction to stereotyping and scapegoating. Let's review these two words and watch them in action.

Stereotyping

Stereotyping is oversimplified generalization about some aspect of reality. Negative stereotyping, the usual type of oversimplifying about a particular group, race, or sex, causes hurt. The following are examples of some of the ways people stereotype others.

Allison, seventeen

"I was over at a friend's house when her Mormon boyfriend came to visit. He said he was leaving for 'Jewtah.' I asked him why he calls Utah that. He said, 'Because I hate Jews.' I asked him to repeat what he had just said. Then I told him I was Jewish and walked out of the room. My friend followed me and said her boyfriend had no idea I was Jewish, and she was sorry. 'No big deal,' I said, but I wondered what gave him the right to say that. We went back in, and she yelled at him and told him to leave. The incident made me think twice about Mormons. But then just last weekend I stayed overnight with a Mormon friend. When we went out, she brought along several other Mormons, and we all had a lot of fun together."

Allison resisted the impulse to counter stereotyping with more stereotyping. She could have said, "I don't like Mormons." Instead, she got to know the people involved on an individual basis.

John, seventeen

"I'm Puerto Rican. I was working at a grocery store when a group of boys came in. They started asking me where my friend Ricky Ricardo was. I said I didn't think they were funny. I called the manager, who made them leave. Whenever I let myself think about it, I still feel mad. As a result, I'm a little quieter and more shy in groups than most people."

Angie, seventeen

"A large group of my classmates, mostly males, discounted my knowledge of a subject [the Supreme Court] because I was 'just a woman.' In addition, I'm Hispanic. During this particular argument, I found a reference book to prove my statement was correct. The males in the room laughed it off. They said my being correct was like winning the lottery: Sometimes you just get lucky. Afterwards I felt proud that

I had taken action to defend myself, and that I was right. When in male company, I usually think before I speak, so that I know I'm correct. If I'm wrong, I add fuel to their sexist fire."

Craig, fifteen

"I enjoy heavy metal music, and I like to hang out with my friends on the hill. In front of the whole class, my science teacher made me out to be a drug addict when actually I've never touched *any* drug. It was just the fact that I had long hair and so did my friends. I used to think my science teacher was a good guy, but ever since he made that comment, I haven't been able to stand looking at him."

Jon, seventeen

"I'm quarterback on the football team at school, and I get along pretty well with the rest of the guys. At least, they seem to like me. But it really hurts when they start talking contemptuously about gays. 'That fag,' they'll say, 'what's he doing in this school?' I wonder what would happen if they knew I had been aware of my homosexuality from the time I entered high school."

Kim, fourteen

"I was shopping with friends, and we stopped for lunch. The waitress was friendly to all the adults in the restaurant but hardly looked at us. She treated us rudely and served us very slowly."

Brad, sixteen

"My Spanish teacher knew I played sports, so he called me 'Jocko' all the time. He didn't treat me as fairly as he treated the other students. I dealt with it by dropping out of the class. Then I never had to see him again."

Ingrid, thirteen

"My brother is seventeen, and my parents are divorced, so my mother asks for my brother's help in driving me places. My softball practices used to be up north, but now they're down south. No matter which place my brother takes me, he says he doesn't want to because the people who live there are hicks, and all the girls who play softball are fat and ugly."

Scapegoating: The Blame Game

Stereotyping often leads to scapegoating. This term originated in the Bible. Leviticus 16:8–22 tells of an ancient Hebrew ritual on the Day of Atonement when the high priest put his hands on a goat's head and confessed the sins of the children of Israel. By this ritual, the sins of the people were transferred to the goat, which was then let go in the wilderness. The people felt guilt-free.

Scapegoating is deliberately placing blame on a certain person or group when the fault lies elsewhere. Scapegoating often makes prominent news headlines. For example, the United States blames illegal aliens for its unemployment problems; Americans blame Japanese car manufacturers for the unhealthy state of the U.S. auto industry. When scapegoating, we don't bother to reason things out. The report of the Civil Rights Commission (mentioned in Chapter 1) called on politicians and others to stop "Japan-bashing." America should face its problems head-on instead of trying to lay them at the doorstep of another country. The following are examples of students' experiences with scapegoating.

Jerome, seventeen

"Our school, Rivertree, has lots of rich kids. Often at debate tournaments the judges deliberately vote against Rivertree because they think we're too good or something. It really isn't fair to lose because you're too good. At this one tournament I knew I should have won; afterwards, I felt angry and upset at the judges."

An objective observer might have reported Jerome's scores as rather low, but it made him feel better to persuade himself that the judges didn't like him or his school. Jerome scapegoated the judges.

Zach, fifteen

"My father owns a used car lot and has many minority customers. He calls blacks 'niggers' and other unkind words. I often get into shouting matches with him over names that should never be spoken. I think I'm tangled in an ignorant suburban web of bias and prejudice."

Adam, fifteen

"When we lived in Texas, I was really good friends with this kid. One day he found out I was Jewish.

For a long time afterward whenever I went to his house, his mom said he was busy. Finally he told me his parents said he wasn't supposed to be friends with Jews."

Damien, sixteen

"I was at this convenience store with a couple of friends. The clerk reacted out of the stereotypic belief that a group of black kids must be gang members out to rob any white-owned business. He accused us of trying to steal and said, 'Get out of my store, niggas.' I started to react with anger but decided to talk philosophically to test his intelligence. I asked why he held such an opinion of blacks. He didn't answer. I guess it was his upbringing, stuff he heard at home. The incident wasn't resolved, and I never went to that store again. The problem with the races is that we don't know anything about each other or our pasts. Each of us thinks his race is superior to all others."

As people get older and begin to think for themselves, they may shake off some of the biases that originated in the family. Kate seems to have tried to do just that.

Kate, sixteen

"My mom and I were walking in a shopping mall, and we saw a white girl and a black guy holding hands. Mom turned to me and said, 'I don't want you *ever* to do that!' I tried to explain my feelings about her opinion, but I was too shocked to get into an argument with her at the time. Afterward I didn't

respect my mom as much. This happened about two
years ago. Since then, whenever I have the chance, I
try to educate my mom about prejudice."

Life experiences, personality factors, and family upbringing may cause a person to become less prejudiced—
or, in some cases, more so.

"No, Sir! Yes, Ma'am!"

Gordon Allport says that the way a child is raised has
something to do with whether or not that child grows up
prejudiced. Parents who are critical, who are stern,
and who demand absolute obedience are more likely to
raise prejudiced children. If a child disobeys such harsh
parents and feels that they are withholding their love
when he is "bad," he learns not to trust others. He learns
that power and authority are of utmost importance. He
feels alone and tends to dislike himself. Those who dislike
themselves, dislike others. Therefore, rejecting parents
seem to have more biased children than do accepting
parents.

Desire for Status

Another possible cause of bias is the need most human
beings have to feel important.

Megan, fifteen

"I was walking in the mall wearing my school sweatshirt, and some girl shouted out that I was a rich
snob. 'If I were you,' she said, 'I'd stop flaunting my
money.'"

We may not know why Megan wore the sweatshirt bearing the name of her affluent high school that day. On the other hand, why shouldn't she wear her school sweatshirt? We don't know if the young woman who shouted at Megan envied the status the sweatshirt implied. We do know that all people crave praise and acceptance. We compete with each other for recognition. Envy and the resulting prejudice are the frequent result.

Gilbert, fourteen

"I was bused to an inner-city school for a gifted and talented program. The school population was 85 percent Hispanic. The kids were always getting on my case because I was white. I'm pretty smart, which compounded my problem. Everyone placed a stereotype on the intelligent white kids: We must all be rich. I'm not rich, but people were always stealing my stuff. I guess some people thought I had too much."

Cari, thirteen

"Lots of times people seem to feel prejudiced against me. I live in a very nice neighborhood with very nice clothes and cars and even a nice house. I guess I *am* sort of spoiled. No wonder people hate me."

IN-GROUPS AND OUT-GROUPS

In-Groups

All of us are members of in-groups. Our immediate family constitutes one such group. Usually a child considers himself a member of his parents' group. In some societies, this membership is firm and unwavering. In the United States, adult children are more likely to give up some parental loyalties and choose new ones. Nevertheless, participation in in-groups gives us a feeling of belonging, which is vital to our mental health. Our daily routines are based on our membership in these comforting groups. Cincinnatians, for example, have loyalties to the Cincinnati Bengals (professional football team), the Cincinnati Bearcats (college team), and the Cincinnati Reds (professional baseball team). When you belong to an in-group, you use the word "we" in describing your group's activities.

Betty, a high school senior, lists the following as some of her in-groups:

Her mother, father, and brother
Her boyfriend
The relatives on her mom's side
The relatives on her dad's side
Her friends in high school
Her neighbors
The residents of her city
The residents of her state
The sisterhood of females

Although your list may be different from Betty's, you certainly have in-group loyalties. Allport suggests that an understanding of our in-group loyalties is important to an understanding of the development of prejudice. We do not necessarily express hostility to out-groups, but the potential exists.

Remember Megan who wore her school sweatshirt to the mall? She explained that her parents had just divorced; the most intimate in-group of her life had split apart.

Wearing her school sweatshirt and meeting up that day with two other girls from her school made her feel less lonely and more a part of a group. She was a member of a solid institution, her school, which had existed since its founding in 1957.

Leslie, fifteen

"I was with my all-white church group at a recreation center in a black neighborhood. We had offered to help do some painting, and we wanted everything to be nice. As soon as we walked into the main hall, we heard remarks, such as 'Look at all those white people' and 'Stupid white girls.'"

Leslie felt as if she were walking on tiptoes and that she should whisper in the center instead of talking out loud. She hoped her church group would not be the cause of further trouble. At the same time, she felt disappointed, offended, and angry. After all, they had come to help. Leslie and the leaders of her group didn't realize that the people at the recreation center felt threatened by their presence. Those on the home turf suddenly felt invaded by members of an out-group.

Out-Groups

Allport says that whenever we have an in-group, we also have a corresponding out-group. Normally these opposing groups don't clash. As members of the Martin family, we don't expect to fight with members of the Brown family, the Walker family, or the Peterson family. Those who receive prejudice from others, however, are likely to give prejudice in return.

Nicole, fifteen

"In elementary school and middle school I lived in a mostly black neighborhood. I was bused to a school in a white neighborhood. I was the only white kid on the bus. Every day coming home from school, people pushed me and yelled at me. The most hurtful name was 'white b—' when I had done nothing to provoke this treatment. I felt upset, but I didn't want to make a big deal about it because I was scared. Also, I felt like maybe I deserved bad treatment because blacks have been oppressed for so long. Maybe this helped make them feel better. I mean, to be able to discriminate against someone who was like those who had discriminated against them. Catch my drift?"

Hanging Out with Prejudiced People

Young people who have been raised with prejudice are likely to seek out others with biased views. These people then make up a prejudiced in-group. Most likely these people have not examined their biases as Nicole did. In the example that follows, a young person is suddenly faced with the need for self-examination.

Stephanie, fifteen

"I was in Jamaica with my family. Almost all the people there were black. On New Year's Day my brother and I went to the beach. It so happened that we were the only whites there. Everyone around us was having a great time, but we couldn't join in because we felt so odd. For the first time in my life, I sensed how it must feel for blacks in a mostly white community. I gave a lot of thought to how all minorities must feel in the neighborhood where I live."

The Importance of Language

Earlier we talked about categories as boxes for sorting things out. In language, too, we make generalizations and put people in boxes. These generalizations can be harmful and hurtful, especially if we are lazy in our thinking. For example we might say, "That black kid gave me a funny look." What we often fail to realize is that there is much more to a person than the color of his skin, his gender, his religion, or his sexual orientation. He is someone's son and someone else's grandson. And yet we categorize him as "black." This kind of labeling can be dangerous. Some people do the same thing with Jews, Catholics, and Polish people. How about trash collectors, blondes, and nerds?

Melissa, fourteen

"Some people hear the word 'Mormon' and seem to get a certain picture in their minds. They must think we practice polygamy or that Mormons are the world's largest religious cult. Also, lots of people call me 'prude.'"

David, fifteen

"I was on a class trip at a skating rink. At the time I went to a Jewish school. This skinhead put a stereotype on all of us. He told me he'd heard all Jews were rich snots. I didn't know what to say, so I said nothing. One of the female chaperones heard him and said, "I've heard all skinheads are stupid. I'm not rich. Are you stupid?' That might not have been the perfect way to deal with the situation, but it sure shut the guy up."

David's tormentor refused to look at the individual characteristics of the students. He stereotyped with a language tag. The adult chaperone tried to wake him up by using a stereotype in return. Can you think of any other way the chaperone might have responded? She might have taken the tormentor aside and said something like this: "I can see you're angry about something, but please don't put labels on my students; it hurts their feelings."

Helen, eighteen

"I was a new student in an elementary school in which most of the other students were Hispanic. I guess they'd never been around black people before. Every day after school they teased my sister and me. They called us 'nigras,' 'los chocolates,' and 'monkeys.'"

Another example of labeling. The majority of the students made no effort to get to know Helen and her sister as people with unique characteristics. Instead they labeled. In this instance, a sensitive teacher could have called all parties together for a meeting. If this action didn't stop the name-calling, perhaps Helen's parents could have demanded a brainstorming session about what to do.

The book *Anti-Bias Curriculum* by Louise Derman-Sparks and others is for those who work with young children, but its message is important for people of all ages. The authors say that what human beings have in common is much more important than their differences, such as variations in skin color or hair texture.

They point out that people's language is such a habit that few see the hurtfulness it can inflict. Take the expression, "No way, José." What about "Indian-giver"? Have you ever thought that these expressions could hurt those being stereotyped? What about, "You fag"? Has it every occurred to you that the person you've addressed in this way could actually be homosexual?

The book suggests "activism" as a response to bias. Activism means standing up for your rights as a human being. The authors describe a situation in which a teacher observed that "flesh-colored" bandages matched the skin of only a small proportion of the children. Activism in this case involved writing to the bandage company to protest. The manufacturer wrote back, suggesting the use of transparent bandages! You may not always get the desired result, but you will at least feel better for having spoken up.

On the other hand, it was recently reported that Crayola, which had originally labeled a light crayon "flesh," is now selling a "Multicultural Pack." Perhaps in response to demand, the crayon company included six colors representing various skin tones plus black and white crayons for blending purposes.

Kent and Jeff

Kent and Jeff are thirteen-year-olds on a Police Athletic League basketball team. Driving them to a game in a predominantly Hispanic neighborhood, Jeff's father couldn't believe the talk coming from the back seat. They boys spoke gibberish with a fake Spanish accent, they joked about tortillas and burritos, and they yelled racial slurs out the window. Six blocks from the ball field, Jeff's father pulled to the curb and stopped the car.

"Hey, what's the deal?" asked Jeff. "We're going to be late for the game."

"Maybe so," said Jeff's father. "But I want to find out if you understand what you've been saying."

"We're just having fun," said Kent. "We didn't mean to make anyone mad."

Jeff's father looked from one gloomy face to the other. "Don't you guys understand that words can hurt? Do you realize there will be Hispanic boys on the team you're playing against today?"

"Actually," said Jeff, "we have some Hispanic boys on *our* team."

Jeff's father nodded. "So how do you think the stuff that's coming out of your mouths would make your teammates feel? How do you think such words would make *you* feel?"

Killing for Shoes

Sometimes economic frustration, unemployment, and the perceived inability to meet needs lead to prejudice and violence. Young people in our materialistic society value the things money can buy. Those who kill for athletic jackets and tennis shoes are not killing for clothes; they're killing for status.

The American dream has changed from a chicken in every pot to a Nike on every foot, says Maisha Bennett, president of the Association of Black Pyschologists (*Rocky Moutain News*, August 7, 1992). Bennett goes on to say that this kind of materialism leads to "spiritual bankruptcy" for white and black Americans alike. But black Americans must face "a pervasive ongoing racism" every day. Most black Americans could understand the rage that led to the violence after the Rodney King verdict, whereas most white Americans could not. Bennett says hate crimes increase as unemployment increases and members of various racial groups compete with each other for jobs. Television bombards people with images of what they need to be happy, such as a fancy car, the best clothes, the perfect athletic shoes.

Some people blame the shoe companies and their advertising. The shoe companies respond by charging their critics with racism. Sociologist Elijah Anderson says that poorly educated kids from the inner city are missing a sense of opportunity. They feel the system is closed to them. "And yet they're bombarded with the same cultural apparatus as the white middle class. They don't have the means to attain the things offered and yet they have the same desire."

Maisha Bennett says prisoners she visits in Chicago jails tell her they stabbed, robbed, or murdered "to get stuff." Bennett believes that people must come to realize there is more to life than material possessions. "The emotional, mental, and spiritual sides of a human must grow along with the material."

Not every frustrated person is prejudiced, but a link exists. An intense craving for status seems to lead to a high degree of prejudice.

Fear

Fear and insecurity are often causes of prejudice and bias incidents. Fear of displacement, fear of hunger, fear of unemployment, fear of the unknown: these insecurities feel real to those being crowded by refugees in the Germany of 1992. A tide of asylum-seekers from eastern Europe, Third World countries, and the former Soviet Union poured into Germany, causing more fears—fears that Germany could repeat its history.

Lack of Democratic Values

When we say someone has "democratic values," we mean that the person has respect for individuals and for group differences, and has a commitment to equality. The further away a person moves from this position, the more likely he is to stereotype, scapegoat, and exhibit prejudice toward others who are different from himself and his group.

Janie, twenty-five

"I graduated from Eastridge High School. When I went there, it was a very nice school. But since I graduated, the ethnic mixture has changed. I mean, there's nothing particularly wrong with that, but now there's gangs and other bad stuff. It's just not a safe place anymore."

Janie seems to be apologizing for her view that a change in ethnic mixture has caused a decline in the quality of her alma mater. Is there any *good* such a change in ethnic mixture could have brought to the school?

In July 1992, Presidential hopeful Ross Perot angered some blacks when before a large gathering of black people at the NAACP convention, he referred to them as "you people." Many at the convention believed Perot showed a lack of respect for individual differences.

Lack of Ability to Think Clearly

One of the greatest gifts home or school can give a person is the ability to think clearly. The more "educated" a person is, the better he or she should be at reasoning. This person will not simply accept a statement just because the speaker happens to be an authority. Have you ever seen the bumper sticker, "QUESTION AUTHORITY"? If more people had questioned Hitler, for example, fifty million lives would not have been lost in World War II.

Summary

The origins of bias are many and complex. What we hear and experience in our families, our desire for status (sometimes trying to appear better than another person by putting him or her down), the desire to belong to a group or groups, our tendency to categorize by making generalizations, fear, a lack of democratic values, and the inability to think clearly all contribute to biased attitudes and bias incidents.

CHAPTER 3

Where Does Bias Occur?

As you go through life at home, school, and work, will bias hit you between the eyes or over the head? Let's hope not, but chances are that at some time or other you will experience a bias incident. In this chapter we first consider racial and ethnic bias. Next we show by example other kinds of bias, such as that against religions, gender, sexual orientation, economic class, geographic turf, and age. Bias incidents also occur over disabilities or handicapping conditions.

RACIAL AND ETHNIC BIAS

Marcia, seventeen

Marcia is an athlete and a cheerleader at a small-town high school in Illinois. She is also active in her Baptist church. She remembers a boy calling her "nigger" because she wouldn't let him play with the basketball she was using. In retaliation she called him a "honky b—" and threw the ball at him. Marcia feels this incident was never resolved. "I still hate him," she says, "and any other prejudiced kids who go to my school."

Natasha, seventeen

Natasha is Marcia's best friend. She too is active in sports and cheerleading and sings in the church choir. The incident that sticks in Natasha's mind occurred when she was about ten. "I was playing with white friends on the school grounds when some eighth-grade boys started calling me 'nigger' and 'Aunt Jemima.' At first I felt humiliated, but those feelings quickly turned to frustration and anger. The only thing I could do at the time was to tell my teacher, who in turn told the principal. The boys were called into the office with me, and they apologized.

"None of my experiences with bias have been anything more than name-calling. I don't think prejudice today is as prevalent as it used to be. Most prejudiced people try not to show their biases to the general public because they know those feelings won't be rewarded or praised. I can stand the name-calling, but if anyone threatened my life or health, I might get angry and hurt someone."

Shannon, eighteen

"I'll be walking down the hall, and someone will run into me or I'll accidentally bump into a person. Then that person will call me 'white b---,' or 'racist b---,' or anything else with 'white' preceding it even

though the incident was completely accidental.
It's frustrating because I think a lot of people at
school hold my race against me. They imply that I'm
personally responsible for every action ever taken
against a minority. It bothers me because I want so
much *not* to have people think that about me."

Shannon would probably feel better if she could understand the various degrees of white racism. She is not a
blatant racist because she is careful not to show prejudice.
Without meaning to, however, she participates in white
racism by enjoying the privileges being white bestows.

Gregory, fourteen

"My ancestors are Armenian. We had a party in my
home. This Turkish guy came. He asked my aunt
where she was from. (She doesn't speak English, so
she asked me what he was saying.) The Turkish guy
said Armenians are warmongers. I was shocked. But
when he left, I forgot about it. The next day he
called, and I happened to pick up the phone. He
said, 'Do you know Armenians start wars all the
time, and they lose because they're not smart?'

"I told my mom and dad, and they called him and
told him they never wanted to see him again. My
parents said, 'If you don't stop calling, we'll sue you,
and we'll win because being prejudiced is a serious
thing in the U.S. of A.' I felt bad and really stupid,
and I even cried because I thought he was telling
the truth, but he really was not. I went and saw a
psychiatrist, and we talked it all over, so I'm okay
now."

They Do Not Hate

Two black women who were beaten, doused with lighter fluid, and almost set on fire by two white men say they do not hate. A *Washington Post* story reports that two young men, ages nineteen and twenty-one, were charged with attempted murder, assault with intent to murder and to maim, kidnapping, and attempting to injure a person for racial reasons. Residents of the community in which all four lived said the two men had threatened the generally peaceful coexistence of blacks, whites, Asians, and Hispanics in their neighborhood. After the attack, neighbors marched in protest. They carried signs saying, "Love thy neighbor no matter what color," and, "Stop hating."

A man who helped the women expressed his anger. He believed that although race might have played a part in the incident, the attack was also gender-based. In addition, he said, "It was those guys lashing out at the world."

Blacks Direct Anger at Koreans

In the aftermath of the Rodney King verdict, dozens of Korean-owned businesses in Los Angeles were torched. Korea-town bore the brunt of the huge losses in property damage. Why? African-Americans resented the business loans Koreans had been able to obtain. Also, they believed Koreans exhibited racist behavior by acting suspicious of black customers.

The not-guilty verdict in the King case reminded some blacks of a tragic incident. After a scuffle, a female Korean shop owner had shot a fifteen-year-old black girl in the back of the head. The teenager had allegedly shoplifted

some orange juice. The storekeeper received only proba-
tion in the incident.

After the riots and in an attempt to begin to heal their
differences, Koreans and African-Americans held a joint
Sunday service. Representative Maxine Waters blamed
the media, the President, and the Los Angeles Police
Department. She said that given the conditions of the
inner city, the rioting may have been justified. "A riot,"
she said, "is the voice of the unheard."

Hispanics vs. Russians?

On January 5, 1992, a forty-eight-year-old Russian-
Jewish immigrant was shot and killed in New York as he
struggled with a man attempting to mug his wife. The
Brighton Beach neighborhood is home to about 35,000
Russians. Although the incident was not an ethnic bias
incident per se, Russian teenagers interviewed afterward
said that fights often erupt between them and Hispanic
teenagers.

Racial and Ethnic Bias at the College Level

Problems for students on college campuses may be subtle.
Minority students identify such handicaps as never
having a professor of their ethnicity, rarely hearing the
accomplishments of their race or nationality acknowl-
edged, and finding few students of similar background in
their classes. As a result, minority students often feel
different or isolated or both.

Transculturally or transracially adopted young people
may encounter special problems in college. *Adopted
Child* (March 1989) interviewed four Korean-American
adoptees halfway through their freshman year. These

teenagers, especially those attending small colleges, had to readjust some of their thinking about themselves. Having been raised by non-Asian parents, the four students did not have strong feelings about being Asian. In the area of academic expectations, the students felt pressure to achieve because they were Asian. Karen, a freshman at Willamette University in Salem, Oregon, experienced stereotyping of Asians as quiet and studious.

Being exposed to a larger number of Asians in college made these young women more interested in their heritage. Diantha, a freshman at the University of Vermont, said that although she was interested in Asian culture, she didn't want to be constantly representing it. In college she began to realize for the first time the tendency of people to judge others by appearances.

Racial and Ethnic Bias at the Neighborhood Level

Recent studies have shown blacks and whites increasingly segregated in housing. Nevertheless, the dream still exists of people of different races coexisting in integrated neighborhoods.

In the summer of 1992, the *Detroit News* sponsored a block party with the aim of discussing integration with the two hundred participants who live in a twelve-block area straddling Mack Avenue. Integration, a hope of Martin Luther King, is still an elusive concept. People of various races live side-by-side in relative harmony in this and other interracial neighborhoods across America, but deep down there is "dis-ease." In the Detroit area, residents on both sides of a racial "comfort zone" say that real integration is hard to achieve. The Grosse Pointe side of Mack Avenue is almost all white; the Detroit side is racially mixed but becoming more black as whites leave.

Many people involved in the problem say that dialogue is the first step. Despite differences, residents of both neighborhoods discovered that when they did talk, they shared common values: safety, high property values, quality schools, and good neighbors. In other words, people of both races found they were more alike than different. Summing things up, Wally Green, a black Detroit resident, said it was up to individuals to dismantle their inner hang-ups. "They create their own fears and their own barriers in their own minds," he said. "We have to remove these barriers if we want to remove that fear."

Worldwide Racial and Ethnic Bias

Ethnic bias is not limited to the United States. Incidents are exploding in South Africa, Europe, and various other sites worldwide. Ethnic bias is a world problem.

Nationalism becomes tribalism, and violence results. With the demise of communism, ethnic conflicts that had lain dormant came to life and began to sizzle. Economic disarray, the lack of democratic traditions, and the use of minorities as scapegoats have caused the flames of war to erupt.

Less than fifty years after the defeat of Hitler and Mussolini, many fear the return of fascism. Recently a German report revealed some unsettling developments. The Ku Klux Klan has taken root in German cities, and extremist groups from the United States are boosting Germany's growing neo-Nazi movement. Young people are playing computer games in which Jewish inmates of Nazi death camps are sent to gas chambers. In a very short time, many seem to have forgotten the deaths of more than fifty million people. Some historians see what is happening today as a replay of the events preceding World War I and World War II.

The end result of the madness is death and destruction. In addition, victims and witnesses of violence often suffer consequences throughout their lives. Some suffer from stress-related problems and disorders, which are discussed in Chapter 5.

RELIGIOUS BIAS

When a person's religion leads to belief in brotherhood (or sisterhood) and tolerance of others, it can be a great force for good. When, however, a person is intolerant of the beliefs of others, bias incidents may result.

Ruth, fifteen

"Last year I had one teacher who hated Jews. I always got absence excuses from other teachers for Jewish holidays. But she never failed to mark me absent (unexcused) and gave me Fs when I tried to make up the work."

Bart, seventeen

"When I was growing up, the Hare Krishnas had a temple on the edge of our neighborhood. One summer two kids from our Baptist Bible school got busted for throwing tomatoes at the building."

Sometimes oppression by the "majority" is simply the result of thoughtlessness. Nevertheless, hurt feelings result.

Rachel, fifteen

"In elementary school the other kids made fun of me because I didn't know the words to the Christmas songs. Being Jewish, I had a hard time around Christmas. My mom and a few other Jewish mothers talked to the principal. They tried to point out that for holiday programs songs like 'Frosty the Snowman' were okay, but others such as 'Silent Night' were not. It's still hard for me to go shopping during the Christmas season, even though I've sort of gotten used to all the decorations in the stores. At one major mall they have a menorah, but the Nativity scene is a hundred times bigger."

GENDER-RELATED INCIDENTS

Wendy, sixteen

"I worked all summer as a lifeguard for $4.85 an hour. Part way through the summer, my boss hired a male lifeguard. The new guy was a friend from my boss's fraternity. They paid him $6 an hour. I didn't say anything for fear of losing my job for the rest of the summer and any future summers. But I was angry and lost respect for my boss. I also became aware that men often get paid more than women for the same job."

Emily, sixteen

"I had gotten a job at a bicycle-repair shop. A week later the manager called me into his office to say that a nineteen-year-old male, who needed a job worse than I did, had applied for my job. Therefore, he no longer needed me. I looked the manager in the eye and said I wouldn't want to work in a place that gave men so much power over women."

Tina, fourteen

"My brother is very sexist. He thinks the women in the household should do all the work. I had finished cleaning my room, and he told me to clean his. I don't think so!"

Liz, seventeen

"Guys I go to school with think because I'm female I can't operate a computer as well as they can. Mostly they look you over—your body, that is. I work harder than they do. I try to prove to them that in many cases women can be just as good as men—if not better."

Sexual Harassment

To harass means "to disturb or irritate persistently"; in other words, "to bother." The confirmation hearings on the nomination of Clarence Thomas to the U.S. Supreme Court caused an explosion of sexual harassment complaints after Anita Hill accused the nominee of such harassment.

Sexual harassment can be a problem in the workplace. The entertainment industry, for one, seems vulnerable to such incidents. In a Los Angeles symposium that focused on the problem, actress Christine Lahti told how she turned down roles in certain movies because of sexual stereotyping of women. She also said she once turned down a role because the director made sexual advances to her. Earlier in her career, she had accepted sexual harassment as part of life.

Actor Greg Harrison reported that fifteen years earlier a female casting director had propositioned him. Since then, he has never been offered a role at the network where she still works. Harrison says people don't even discuss the sexual harassment of men by women or by other men because to do so would not be "macho." Panelists at the symposium agreed that harassment of women is likely to increase because men feel threatened by the growing power of women in society.

The military is another place in which sexual harassment seems to occur often. Not long ago a Wyoming woman reported that she had been sexually harassed and raped while in the Navy during the 1960s. A 1990 Pentagon study found that two thirds of U.S. servicewomen had been sexually harassed by male military personnel. Few filed complaints for fear of what would happen to them. In 1992 the House Armed Services Committee conducted two days of hearings on sexual assaults and harassment in the Armed Forces. The issue of sexism in the military burst into the open with the allegation that Navy officers had assaulted at least twenty-six women at the annual Tailhook Convention in 1991.

Sexual harassment can also happen in schools. Eve Hendricks, a State Department of Education consultant, is an authority on the subject. In an interview in the *New York Times* (January 5, 1992), she said that sexual harassment need not be directed at a person. Obscene jokes, offensive pin-up pictures—any sexual incident that makes students nervous about walking down the hall—can create a "chilly climate" and make people feel insecure and out of control. Especially dangerous, says Hendricks, are teachers or other adults who harass kids from a position of power.

Tiffany, seventeen

"I asked my male teacher a question. In front of the whole class he called me a 'dumb blonde.' This went on and on. After putting up with it for a semester, I told my parents. We had a conference with the principal and the teacher. I finally got out of his class. After that I felt better, but I still see him in the halls. He stares me down and makes me feel very small. I just don't feel comfortable when I see him. I think about it a lot."

One of the reasons sexual harassment is so dangerous, says Hendricks, is that it causes students to conclude that the world in general is not a safe place and that the people who are supposed to protect them are not doing so. The results both in schools and in the workplace are profound depression, mistrust, and even antisocial behavior. Hendricks suggests that schools put a grievance procedure in place and that every student be made aware of it. Another thing every student should know is that every human being deserves to be treated with respect and compassion.

A recent report in *Better Homes and Gardens* (August 1992) points out that the U.S. Supreme Court has ruled that students have the right be sue their school for damages caused by sexual harassment. In Chaska, Minnesota, a high school was faulted for failing to consider seriously a complaint against male students who circulated a list of the twenty-five girls with whom they would most like to have sexual intercourse. (For those who would like to know how to better cope with sexual harassment, help is available. To order *Tune In to Your Rights: A Guide for Teenagers About Turning Off Sexual Harassment*, send $3 by check or money order payable to "University of Michigan" to: Tune In—PEO, 1005 School of Education, Dept. BHG, University of Michigan, Ann Arbor, MI 48109-1259.)

Date and Acquaintance Rape

Rape is a crime of violence motivated by the desire to control and dominate. In the United States a rape occurs every six minutes. Although exact definitions of rape vary from state to state, forced sexual acts are considered rape. Acquaintance rape is forced sexual intercourse or other sexual acts that occur between people who know each other. Date rape is forced sexual intercourse or other sexual acts that occur in a dating situation. Alcohol is often a factor in acquaintance or date rape. A man may be more likely to commit rape if he has been drinking. On the other hand, a woman who avoids consuming alcohol is better able to avoid acquaintance and date rape. According to statistics from former Surgeon General Antonia Novello, alcohol is a factor in more than half the rapes involving college-age students.

Myth: Rapists usually attack strangers.
Fact: Acquaintances of the victim commit 80 percent of rapes. Strangers commit only 20 percent.

Myth: Rape usually involves college-age people.

Fact: Three in five sexual assaults occur when victims are seventeen or younger. Nearly three in ten occur when the victim is ten or younger.

In a recent newspaper story, a five-year-old girl identified an eight-year-old boy and a twelve-year-old boy who had undressed her and tried to have sex with her.

Myth: Most victims report sexual assaults.

Fact: Only 14 percent of rape victims report the crime to the police.

Myth: Most young men believe rape is a crime.

Fact: A recent survey showed that 86 percent of sixth-grade boys believed it would be okay to demand sex from a girl if the boy had spent money on her.

A three-year study by the National Victims Center concluded that 12.1 million women in the United States (or one in eight) have been rape victims.

In another three-year study, researcher Cindy Carosella looked at the long-term effects of rape. None of the twenty women Carosella interviewed had pressed charges against the rapist for fear of being blamed.

In New York, two men allegedly abducted and raped a fifteen-year-old girl as she waited for a bus to school. Because the victim was white and the attackers were black, police treated the assault as a bias incident. The men told the victim they chose her because she was "white and perfect." The then Police Commissioner Lee P. Brown said that although rape is always a horrible and cowardly act, it is more so when two men act together against a schoolgirl. "Add to rape the element of racial bias, and you have an unspeakable crime that is offensive to every decent man and woman."

More Violence Against Women

Rape is one example of violence, but teenagers sometimes find themselves in abusive relationships that include verbal assaults and various forms of physical abuse. Many young people experience violence in their homes and communities.

A woman is battered in the United States every fifteen seconds. According to the Surgeon General, battering is the single most common cause of injury to women, greater than muggings, rape, and car accidents combined.

Family violence experts suspect that one out of four high school students is involved in a violent relationship. Most incidents involve young men abusing their girl-friends. Girls tend to hit back in self-defense; young men are more likely to use violence to intimidate. Shouting, threatening, or intentionally humiliating a person are all forms of violence and may serve as a warning of physical violence to come.

Where do young people learn these kinds of actions? Parents, the media, and peers often model "macho" behavior. If you're a "real man," you will be aggressive and tough. Researchers Rosenbaum and O'Leary found that 75 percent of young males in abusive relationships had abusive parents. In contrast only 25 percent of young women in such relationships came from abusive homes.

Often the abuse takes the form of a cycle, with the abusive person showing much remorse after the incident. The abused person tends to forgive and tries to forget, hoping the abuser has finally changed. Instead, the cycle usually repeats, with the abuse being worse the next time.

Counselors advise anyone who has suffered such abuse to tell someone. Getting help is the first step in solving the problem.

Reproductive Freedom

The World Health Organization recently reported that worldwide an average of one woman a minute dies from complications of pregnancy or childbirth. The agency's report, *Reproductive Health, a Key to a Brighter Future*, says that access to contraception has increased around the world in the past few decades, giving women more control over their bodies and their lives. Women need to be able to control their fertility in order to complete their education, maintain employment, and in general have "women's rights."

Homosexuality

If heterosexual women have a hard time in our society, homosexual males and females have an even harder time. *Denver Post* reporter Maureen Harrington interviewed gay young people who agree with Natasha, quoted in Chapter 3. Name-calling they can handle. Faggot, queer, gay. Lez, dyke, homo. But the high school years for these teens are not the best years of their lives. Some get slammed against lockers. One girl found the word "dyke" written on her car. A nineteen-year-old says it's safer out on the streets than in high school.

The National Gay and Lesbian Task Force Policy Institute reports that antigay violence increased by 31 percent between 1990 and 1991. Teens who are gay may retreat into alcohol and drugs. Between 30 and 40 percent of homeless and runaway teens are gay. Gay teens commit approximately one third of all suicides. Bruce Guernsey, director of Denver's school-based clinics, observes, "To be gay and a teen is really hard. The grief the kids get is a reflection, I think, of the larger society. We're not very tolerant."

Crystal, seventeen

In spite of hassling for being Hispanic and gay, Crystal will be attending college on scholarships. She graduated from high school with a 3.9 grade-point average. Crystal gives her mother credit for pushing her, making her do her homework, and keeping her away from gangs. But she considers her mother's support of her homosexuality unusual. She knows gay teens who have been locked out and disowned by their parents. She can understand why many want to commit suicide. She herself has been beaten up and locked in a gym locker. In spite of evidence that young people are becoming less understanding of differences, Crystal, armed with a good education and support from home, looks forward with hope to the future.

"*2 Get 25 Years to Life in Gay Man's Slaying in Queens.*" This headline in the *New York Times* (January 11, 1992) tells only part of the story. In July 1990, Daniel Doyle and two other young men killed Julio Rivera "because he was gay." Doyle testified against his friends. The three of them had worked together in the crime. The other two lured Rivera into an isolated corner of a schoolyard and beat him savagely with a hammer and a beer bottle. Then Doyle stabbed him to death.

According to the news story, Doyle, a high-achieving college student, was also the leader of a skinhead gang. Although Doyle said he was sorry, Rivera's brother had no forgiveness. "My brother will never come back; I will never speak to him again." The judge who sentenced Doyle to prison for first-degree manslaughter told him, "You and people who think like you are a disgrace to the human race."

ECONOMIC/CLASS BIAS

Economic/class bias is hard to pin down but can be seen and heard in subtle ways:

- "My brother and I were downtown with my father's clients (in the *bad* part), and these Mexican kids hassled us."
- "We went to this black, lower-class neighborhood and . . ."

The speakers look down on those who have less than they do and seem to equate this "have not" status with race or ethnicity.

Chet Whye, president of a high-tech engineering firm, says that economic bias is one of the most difficult to overcome. Large companies, Whye says, are reluctant to hire black engineers; he calls this "blatant racism."

In *Children of the Dream: The Psychology of Black Success*, authors Audrey Edwards and Craig Polite say that in a society in which whites have had a 200-year head start, race is still an economic factor. Another writer, Jim Wallis, says that the most visible and painful sign of the continuation of racism is the gross economic inequality between blacks and whites. Originally racism justified slavery, which yielded great economic benefits for whites. Says Wallis, "The heart of racism was and is economic . . ." In the years between 1970 and 1980, the economic gap between whites and most blacks widened. In inner-city neighborhoods, rage results from unemployment. Poverty and lost hope translate into substance abuse, crime, and family disintegration. "That blacks are disproportionately consigned to the lowest economic tier is an indisputable proof of racism," says Wallis.

Gordon Allport points out that economic needs, such as the need for a job, clothes, shelter, and food, also translate into needs for self-esteem, status, and prestige. In other words, long after a person has met his basic needs, he still craves status. He wants to be "on top" or at least higher on the success ladder than he is.

Vanessa, fourteen

"People always think that because my dad's a doctor and my mother's a nurse, we're rich. That is not true. My family is probably better off than some, but . . ."

Vanessa's comment shows how aware even young people are of status, and how people tend to pigeonhole others as to income.

In discussing why kids kill for a pair of tennis shoes or other articles of clothing, black film-maker and actor Spike Lee says, "Let's try to effectively deal with the condition that makes a kid put so much importance on a pair of sneakers, a jacket and gold. These kids feel they have no options, no opportunities."

The same week Julio Rivera lost his life "because he was gay," a nineteen-year-old New York youth on an errand for his mother was shot to death for a leather coat he'd received as a Christmas present. A police officer commented, "From what I'm assuming, he was getting robbed for his coat. I think after he surrendered it, he was shot in the head."

Frustration at economic circumstances can lead to bias incidents. Young people who see themselves going nowhere often look for someone to scapegoat. Troubles then arise for economic rather than racial reasons.

Associated Press reporter Arlene Levinson says that racism costs America big money. Many of the nation's thirty million blacks find business loans hard to get. Often, well-educated African-Americans find roadblocks in their way toward advancement. Edward Irons, dean of business at Clark Atlanta University, recently said, "Unless we get a handle on racism, foreign competitors are going to eat our lunch."

TURF BIAS

Turf battles cause gang warfare, another kind of bias incident. Historically, gangs formed to defend a group's neighborhood from outsiders. Today rival gangs fight each other, and their warfare escalates with ever more deadly weapons. Armed gangs are often involved in drug deals. Random shootings in rival territory kill innocent people.

> **Myth:** In the United States, gangs are a new phenomenon.
> **Fact:** Youth gangs have been around for a long time. The residents of Philadelphia battled

gangs in 1791, and New York City had gang problems as early as 1825. Today, however, gangs are more dangerous because of the easy accessibility of sophisticated weapons.

Myth: Gang members are almost always males in their late teens.

Fact: These days gang members tend to be much younger. Children as young as seven or eight identify themselves with the gang of an older relative. Ten-year-olds run errands and carry weapons for older gang members. Girls are also gang members.

Myth: Gang violence usually occurs between members of different ethnic groups.

Fact: Studies show that gang violence usually occurs between rival groups of the same ethnic or racial background.

According to *Gangs in Schools: Breaking Up Is Hard to Do*, by the National School Safety Center, today's dominant ethnic gangs are made up of Hispanic, African-American, and Asian young people. Increasingly prominent are white "stoner" gangs, whose members are usually fans of heavy metal music, often use drugs, and sometimes are involved in satan worship. Some of these gangs advocate white supremacy.

The Albanian Boys Inc. (or Albanian Bad Boys, as they are sometimes called) is an ethnic gang in New York that has claimed responsibility for bias incidents. Some say the Bad Boys began as a group of young people sharing neighborhood and family ties. Although they liked to stir things up, former members deny racial or ethnic bias. In the early days at least, they say they just wanted to earn a reputation for being bad.

Why do young people get involved with gangs? For the same reason anyone joins a group: Groups (even gangs) provide a sense of belonging and companionship in a world that often seems hostile. Sometimes, as in the case of the Bad Boys, negative attention seems better than no attention at all.

Turf bias does not always involve gang membership. Melodie felt that people were biased against her when she moved from Ohio to Massachusetts.

Melodie, fourteen

"My mom was doing an internship, and we had to live in Massachusetts for nine months. I didn't know anyone at the new school. I wanted to make friends, but I didn't talk because I didn't know anyone. I felt like an idiot because I was afraid to stand up for myself. The rats (stoners) always made fun of me because I didn't talk."

Turf battles can take the form of defending your school against all others.

Brent, sixteen

"It hasn't happened just once; it happens all the time. People consider our school a rich kids' school. As soon as they hear the name, they start snickering and making back-handed comments about the 'rich snobs.' Often I feel uncomfortable saying where I'm from. I try to play it down. Sometimes, though, I play it *up* and *act* snobby because I get sick of hearing that stuff."

Charlie, fifteen

"I was in a predominantly black area of the South when a group of African-Americans approached me. They yelled at me and called me a bunch of names and told me to get the heck out of their neighborhood."

In more serious turf battles, bias can lead to death. Two teenagers, nineteen and fifteen, were tried as adults in the kicking death of Army Spec. Layne Schmidtke, twenty-five. Witnesses said Schmidtke and a friend were on their way to a hamburger stand when they passed a crowd of teenagers. Someone in the crowd yelled to the two men to stay off their "turf." When Schmidtke yelled back, a fight began. Schmidtke took thirty to forty kicks to the head. Later that night, he died of his injuries.

AGE BIAS

Many young people report bias incidents having to do with their age.

Lisa, seventeen

"In certain stores when I'm alone or with people my age, clerks are rude or ignore me. But if you have a purse or look rich, or if you're with an adult, they do anything to please you. Their whole intent is for you to spend money, and they assume if you don't look rich or whatever, you aren't going to buy anything."

Brian, fifteen

"A group of teenagers (me included) walked into a convenience store, and immediately an employee came from behind the counter to stand on a stool in the middle of the store. He watched us to make sure nobody shoplifted anything."

Bias Against Those with Disabilities

A large group of young people report suffering from bias because they look or seem "different." A frequent cause of "differentness"is a disabling or handicapping condition.

Paul, fifteen

"I'm hearing-impaired and wear hearing aids. Often people stare at me. It was much worse, though, in the lower grades. Kids thought I was different, and I felt left out."

Mindy, fifteen

"My problem is stammering. At the beginning of the year I gave a report and had trouble speaking. For the rest of the year whenever I talked, almost everyone made fun of me. I felt bad and of less worth than others who talked normally. It's still difficult for me to talk in front of a group. I rarely say anything in class for fear of being ridiculed."

Kurt, fourteen

"Because I have poor eyesight, I've worn glasses since first grade. For that reason, people have always called me a nerd. Since I started high school, though, things have gotten better. My friends have learned it's not my physical appearance that makes me who I am."

Joanne, fourteen

"I was walking into school by myself, and these guys were hanging out of the second-story window. One of them yelled, 'Sexy mama.' A second guy said, 'No, she isn't; she's a blue whale.' This was a comment on my weight. I kept walking but felt mad at myself for being overweight."

Bob, fifteen

'In sixth grade several kids teased me about my weight (I was stocky), about my teeth (I had braces), and about my height (I was short for my age). Luckily, it was all resolved at about fourteen when I got the braces off, caught up to the other kids in height, and lost some weight."

Pete, nineteen

"I remember my first year of junior high. How could I forget it? I was new in the school. My mom had just died, and I had to go live with my dad. I was skinny and dorky. I was the outcast, the kid who didn't fit in. Other kids picked on me and I fought them. It was the worst year of my life."

Sometimes people who are developmentally delayed or mentally slow experience bias. On the other hand, young people who seem "too smart" also suffer from bias.

Sam, fourteen

"I was smarter than the other kids and acted different. My mother said I matured faster. Anyway, when I went into middle school, some of the other kids started messing around with me. Some tripped me or slammed my locker door shut. I knew everyone at the school, but only a few kids said 'Hi' in the halls. I felt alone and stressed out, at times to the extent of getting physically sick. My mother talked about sending me to a different school, but she didn't and I survived. Now in high school things are much better."

Summary

As we can see from the various stories, bias is all around us. Young people experience racial and ethnic bias, religious bias, gender bias, economic/class bias, turf bias, and bias because they are "different." Teens also report suffering from bias incidents for other reasons. One young woman reported that some of her peers were biased against her because she was a hunter. In the next chapter we discuss the ways in which bias is shown.

CHAPTER ◇ 4

Kinds of Bias

G ordon Allport ranks the types of bias incidents in a hierarchy of ascending intensity and violence—talk, avoidance, verbal rejection, discrimination, physical attack, and extermination.

TALK IS CHEAP

Most people have biases. Those who won't admit having biases are probably kidding themselves. Usually people keep their prejudices to themselves or express them only among close friends and relatives. If people admit their biases to themselves and keep their opinions within a small circle of acquaintances, they are unlikely to hurt anyone very much. The danger comes with progression. For example, if talking about someone in a prejudiced way leads to avoidance, and avoidance leads to verbal rejection, and so on up the intensity ladder to violence, a problem exists.

Allport points out that Hitler's speeches caused Germans to avoid their Jewish neighbors, formerly their friends. Later, Germany enacted laws of discrimination that made the burning of synagogues and street attacks on Jews seem natural. The final progression of negative action was to the ovens at Auschwitz.

In the following examples, the talk is quiet and private, the first level of prejudice.

Mary Lee, fifteen

"I was the only white girl on our basketball team. No one ever said anything to me about being white, but I could sense it from certain individuals. I suspect the other team members might have said something about me behind my back. I felt strange and out of place, but as time passed the girls who seemed biased against me began to accept me."

Leon, eighteen

"Maybe I'm paranoid, but I feel that the police, especially the white cops, are always sweating me and thinking about giving me a hard time. Sometimes I definitely feel unwanted. But I try to remember the words of one of my favorite authors—as long as you keep your thoughts free and your imagination free, unwise people can't get to you."

Millicent, sixteen

"I'll admit I've called white people 'honkies' or 'whities,' but I never would use such names in public. I've had a better upbringing than that."

AVOIDANCE

Avoidance is a slightly more intense way of expressing bias or prejudice. The person who is prejudiced may not actually intend to hurt the avoided person, even though the object of the behavior may *feel* hurt. Kerry, a black teenager, reported a subtle form of avoidance. She noticed that some white store clerks put her change on the counter instead of in her hand. One day she stuck around and watched those who followed. She noticed that the Anglos who came next got their change directly in the palm of their hand.

Traci, seventeen

"Every day there's a new incident. One that made me feel particularly bitter happened in my advanced-placement English class. This was an all-Anglo class of thirty people, and no one would sit next to me because I'm black. It's okay. I'm getting the same education they are. My father's income is probably higher than 98 percent of the class, and I have plenty of black friends."

Donna, fifteen

"In seventh grade everyone avoided me. I didn't have any friends because my family was poor. I couldn't buy my clothes from The Gap, so I dressed a little differently. Now in high school some people who knew me in middle school still won't talk to me because of the way I *used* to look. I don't think people should be judged by their clothes."

VERBAL REJECTION

"Sticks and stones may break my bones, but names will never hurt me." Remember that old saying? Those who have experienced name-calling sometimes downplay its impact. And yet, name-calling *does* hurt, and it often leads to more intense bias, such as discrimination. The "hunter" mentioned at the end of the last chapter had to defend herself against verbal rejection.

Lauren, sixteen

"Because I hunt, many people call me 'Bambi Killer' and other such names. This makes me angry. Most people don't understand what hunters do for wildlife. They keep the animal population within the area's carrying capacity, and they pay for a lot of services provided by the wildlife and game department. I try to explain to people how much hunters do for wildlife and that the animals would starve to death without hunters, but most people don't bother to listen to me."

Martin, fourteen

"I'm Chinese-American. One day two big white skinheads came up to me and my friends while we were playing basketball. They told us to leave the court. We refused. They reacted by calling us racial names and pushing us around."

Kristen, fifteen

"My friend and I (both of us black) were at the state science fair. Many other students talked down to us and used racial slurs against us because we were the only blacks in our division. We ignored them because there was nothing else we could do. Experiences like that discourage me from entering such contests; though I love science, I don't like dealing with bias."

Rochelle, fifteen

"A person in my French class made a comment about Jews. Then some people behind me started saying untrue things. I turned around and said, 'Excuse me. I'm Jewish.' The incident was never really resolved. Yes, the people did stop saying rude things about Jews, but I don't think anyone changed."

Verbal bias incidents go on all the time, but on January 12, 1992, the *New York Times* actually reported two examples. On January 10, police in Queens said that a group of white men in a car had shouted racial slurs at a seventeen-year-old Hispanic youth. The next morning on a subway train in Manhattan, three black men followed a twenty-three-year-old white man onto the train, shouted racial slurs, then slapped the young man in the face.

DISCRIMINATION

Discrimination occurs when a person or group denies equal treatment to someone.

Rick, fourteen

"I lived in England for a while. I was teased there because I talked differently. The kids wouldn't let me play some of their games. At first I ignored them. Then I tried to prove I was okay. When that didn't work, I decided I didn't need them as friends. I don't know what you'd call my reactions since then, but I feel lonelier and more depressed than many of my friends. I think about death often."

Stacy, fifteen

"I'm Hispanic and black. People don't like mixed children. Besides, I'm female. I was held back in a work situation because of being a woman. Some of the men got raises. I didn't, and I had seniority. I worked hard to prove I was capable of any assignment. I showed them by my work that I deserved a raise. When they realized they were wrong, they fired me and eliminated my position."

Being of mixed racial heritage and female proved to be more of a handicap on the job than Stacy could overcome. Mira's story shows how stereotyping can lead to discrimination.

Mira, fifteen

"It all happened because of the way I looked. As a seventh grader, my hair was high, and I wore lots of makeup. This one teacher treated me unfairly and put me down a lot. Even when I asked him for help, he refused to take time to help me. His good friend, another teacher, always put me down and predicted my future in a negative way. They constantly told me how I would grow up and drop out of school because my grades were bad. (But they wouldn't take the time to help me.) They predicted I would never have a life, or that I would end up selling myself, or that I'd become majorly suicidal.

"They judged me wrong. I wish I'd had enough guts to stand up for myself, so I wouldn't have followed everyone else to please them. I've always done my best to be honest and caring, but they never looked past my face."

PHYSICAL ATTACK

Going a step further, bias and discrimination can take the form of physical attack. Sometimes the victim can find no reason for the attack.

Jared, fifteen

"I was standing in the lunch line minding my own business when this guy comes up and hits me. I hit him back. Then he starts choking me because I'm not letting him bully me around. Afterward I felt weak and humiliated."

John, fifteen

"I was waiting for a ride at the mall, and three long-haired boys beat me up. I couldn't do a thing about it, they were holding my arms. The abuse ended when a woman pulled up in a car and scared them away."

Sometimes, in spite of complaints to authorities, physical abuse continues.

Roger, fourteen

"When I was in middle school, I was often harassed, physically threatened, and assaulted. Several times I went to the principal and complained. For some reason, he didn't like me and did nothing. When I got to high school, I had more friends, was bigger, and the administration was more caring. I haven't had any problems since."

Todd, thirteen

"I'm Anglo. In fifth grade I went to a magnet school. One day a gang of kids jumped me and pulled off my shoes. I kicked and hollered, but they got my shoes anyway. Then a teacher saw them, so they dropped the shoes. At the time I didn't understand why people angry at an entire race would take out their rage on a single person. I always knew something like that would happen sooner or later, though, because people tend to pick on me because of my color."

Vicki, fifteen

"A few black girls told me that because of my light skin (I'm biracial) and long hair, I thought I was better than them. After they insulted me, they jumped me. I fought back. They got suspended, and I learned to control my temper. Now I tell people they have a right to whatever opinions they might hold."

Mai, fifteen, Vietnamese-American

"I was walking down the street when a couple of kids started throwing rocks at me. They also pretended to speak a different language (I assume it was supposed to be some Asian language). I gave them the dirtiest looks I could make and warned them that if anything hit me, they'd be sorry. I walked on. Apparently those kids couldn't throw long distances. I wished I could have beat them up."

Justin, seventeen

"It started when I was in fourth grade. A Mexican boy and a black boy tried to beat me up for being of a different race. They forced me to do their homework for them. This went on until sixth grade. At the time, I felt lonely and upset. In sixth grade I began to feel better about myself, and I finally told someone, who made them stop. The kids who picked on me now go to high school with me, and we get along better, though I still feel a little hatred."

Faith, sixteen

"This happened in middle school—about seventh grade. I am white, and some people hated me for it. I was smart, too, and good at playing the flute. Some black girls said cruel things to me and even pushed me around a little. I asked some teachers to change my seat, and I stayed away from them, but . . . I can't say it was ever resolved. They eventually got tired of bothering me, but no one ever said anything. We just accepted it and let it pass. I like people for who they are, and I'm sorry if people can't view me that way."

Carolyn, sixteen, biracial

"During the parade for Martin Luther King Day, the Ku Klux Klan was demonstrating at the capitol. I went to look at them. As the bus was leaving with the KKK members, some marchers in the parade threw snowballs at it. The police started to lash out against the crowd. They threw teargas and hit people with billy clubs. The cops made human barricades and brought out dogs. This was an almost all-black crowd with an entirely white police force. I was 'hit' by a horse, teargassed, and blocked from entering the downtown of my own city. I felt more angry than I ever had before. I keep this incident in mind to motivate me to overcome the society that has managed to oppress African-Americans for more than three hundred years."

In dealing with the types of bias we've discussed so far—verbal rejection, discrimination, physical attack—don't react; defuse. If you let it happen, any of these bias incidents can cause hurt and diminished self-esteem. However, you do not have to kiss your self-respect good-bye. Simply practice a technique known as defusing. Imagine a lighted fuse. An explosion could result. Your job is to 'defuse.' The defusing will be a small "poof" and will leave your opponent feeling like a popped balloon. The following examples show defusing in action.

Racist
statement: "No Mexican ever amounted to anything."

Response: "You must have quite an extensive knowledge of Mexico."

Abusive statement: "You talk funny."

Response: "My speech must sound unusual to you."

Abusive statement: "You'll never get a life."

Response: "You must not approve of my life-style."

Abusive statement: "Hey, Mafia Mama! Do you eat spaghetti for breakfast?"

Response: "I love pasta. Have you ever tried it with clam sauce?"

Because the targeted person fails to blow up, the attacker looks a bit silly. Thinking up creative defusers can be a great intellectual exercise. The sky's the limit. If you have a hard time thinking on your feet or in crisis situations, invent some possible defusers ahead of time. Then plan and practice your responses. Role playing is discussed in Chapter 5.

EXTERMINATION

The final type of bias incident is extermination. The word "holocaust" means "widespread destruction." The Holocaust has come to mean the widespread destruction of the Jewish people during World War II. Before the war ended in 1945, the Germans had killed more than six million of the ten million Jews in Europe. That is extermination. The specter is so horrible that many people cannot comprehend it. Some even attempt to deny its reality.

Becca, fifteen, Jewish

"This guy yelled at me that the Holocaust never happened. I asked him how six million Jews died if the Holocaust never happened. He didn't reply."

Anti-Semitism has been called "the disease that won't die." Columnist Cal Thomas writes that the new generation that did not live through the period of the Holocaust, or the formation of the Israeli state as a haven for the Jewish people, is being exposed on some college campuses to watered-down ideas about the Holocaust. "These are nothing more than regurgitated myths that the Holocaust never happened and was simply made up by Jews to gain sympathy . . ."

Denial also exists of the persecution of homosexuals in Nazi Germany. The Protestant Church of Austria estimates that more than 200,000 homosexual men were persecuted and killed during the Holocaust.

Recent reports show a different kind of extermination of homosexual men and women by the military of the United States. In the past ten years, the Pentagon has spent approximately half a billion dollars replacing men and women who had been forced from the service because of their sexual orientation. In the recent past, the military has discharged an average of 1,500 people a year because they are gay.

Violence

Another threat to existence (extermination) is our current culture of violence—gunfights, knifings, bludgeonings, murder.

One summer evening Jorge Olivas and his younger

brother, Genaro, were driving their children to McDonald's. Jorge now says he wishes he had ignored the racial slur, "Wetback." When he stopped, someone put a 0.25-caliber automatic pistol between his eyes and said, "Look what I have." This was not the first time the Olivas brothers, both from Mexico, had run into prejudice from either Anglos or Hispanics. "I've been called names— wetback and worse—before," Jorge says. "I always just ignore it." This time when Jorge pulled away in his car, a seventeen-year-old Hispanic youth fired three shots; one hit Genaro in the forehead. The authorities attribute the shooting to macho behavior, gang mentality, and prejudice. Hispanics who have been around a while tend to look down on new arrivals. For now, Genaro's family just hope he'll recover.

Some of these incidents are even happening in schools. According to the National School Safety Center, three million incidents of theft, assault, rape, and robbery take place in schools every year. Gunfights have replaced fistfights.

One way to cut down on the violence would be to decrease the accessibility of weapons. But that is not an easy task in the United States. If you are interested in helping with handgun control, write to Handgun Control, Inc., 1225 Eye Street, NW, Room 1100, Washington, DC 20005, or call 1-202-898-0792.

Can't we all get along? The alternative is mass destruction/extermination. Keep in mind that not all people of color are violently angry, and many whites aspire to be nonracists. Mayor David Dinkins of New York says, "Violence begets violence, hate begets hate." Revenge and vigilantism, he adds, will not help fix anything. "It is said that an eye for an eye and a tooth for a tooth will leave everyone blind and toothless." Pastor Phil

Campbell concurs, "We either learn to live together as [sisters and] brothers or we perish together as fools."

Summary

So far, political leaders and concerned citizens have had difficulty finding solutions to the problems of bias in our society. We seem more clear on what the answers are not than on what they are.

Most young people have enough trouble dealing with individual incidents that present themselves in everyday life. If you are involved in a bias incident, how do you cope? The next chapter offers some suggestions.

CHAPTER 5

Handling Bias Incidents

Mike's Meeting

Mike is fourteen. His mother is white; his father is black. Mike is an honor-roll student in eighth grade. His best friend, Andy, is white. Both are members of the First Presbyterian Church, which has an active youth program.

At the beginning of the school year, four boys started giving Mike and Andy a hard time. The ringleader of the bullies was Larry, who is of black and Hispanic background. Larry is not as good a student as Mike. He envies the attention Mike gets at school for being an all-around good kid.

One day while walking home from school on a gravel path, Mike and Andy had a rock-throwing contest. No one else was around. Suddenly Mike felt himself hurtling through the air from a hard push on the back. Beside him, Andy struggled to get up.

When both boys got their feet on the ground, they faced Larry.

"What's going on?" Mike asked.

"Why were you guys throwing rocks at me?" Larry said in a voice as low as a growl.

"We weren't," Andy said.

Mike gave Andy a nudge. "Come on. Let's go." Mike had the sense not to argue with Larry, but he was angry. His feelings were hurt, and so were his hands, which stung from the imprint of the gravel.

At home, Mike told his mother what had happened. "What do you think you should do?" she asked.

William Ury, author of *Getting Past No: Negotiating with Difficult People*, says that when confronted with a difficult situation, people tend to react without thinking. A first reaction, to strike back, is normal, but it may make the situation worse.

Mike's Situation

Mike and Andy could have beaten Larry up, but that reaction would not have improved anything. Later, Larry would have found a way to escalate the conflict.

A second reaction could have been to give in and let Larry win. This would no doubt have had the unwanted result of making Mike and Andy feel like victims. For example, they could have considered themselves beaten and waited for the next attack from Larry and his bully friends.

A third reaction is to avoid the person who has attacked you. With a truly biased person, this may be the only sensible way to behave; no good is likely come of tangling with this person. But what if you are in the same school or class and have to see the person every day? Mike and Andy were in Larry's physical education class. You don't get anywhere, and your opponent holds the power.

Ury gives five tips for getting past your opponent's anger or fear. First, learn not to react. If you react, you lose your objectivity, the trait you need for thinking straight. A reaction from you is what your opponent wants. Instead, get away from the situation, mentally, physically, or both. Before you do anything, buy yourself some time.

Mike bought himself some time by *not* reacting. He didn't slug Larry, nor did he throw something at him. He didn't even talk to him. He dropped all action until he could discuss the situation with his parents.

Second, you must figure out how to disarm your attacker. Trying to reason with him will only make him more angry. Disarming means finding a way to get him to listen to your point of view. Surprise is the key. You must do the opposite of what he expects.

The next day in the hall at school, Mike went up to Larry. "Hi, how's it going?" he asked. Larry found himself off-guard, not knowing what to do next. On the other hand, Mike felt secure. He had a plan. After talking the situation over with his parents, Mike had decided to report the incident to school authorities. He asked the counselor if he and Andy could have a face-to-face meeting with Larry.

Third, change the game. Do the opposite of what you instinctively feel like doing. Focus on the problem by asking problem-solving questions. Try asking your opponent what he or she would do to solve the problem.

Mike's first-hour teacher and the counselor invited the three boys to a morning meeting. Mike took the offensive—in a nice way. "Help me figure out what's happening," Mike said. (His mother had helped him rehearse his lines.) Larry didn't reply. Mike made sure to keep his voice calm and quiet. "What if we keep battling each other?" asked Mike. "What good is that going to do? What are we going to accomplish?"

Fourth, help your opponent say yes by asking for ideas or offering a choice.

Mike suggested to Larry that they *could* find a solution to their conflict. During this stage of the meeting, Larry revealed some of his feelings of inferiority. He said he had known Mike since grade school and had tried to make friends with him, but Mike had always preferred to run around with his "white friend." He also said that he envied the attention Mike received for his friendliness to everyone and his good grades. Larry was strong and athletic, but no one ever seemed to notice him.

Fifth and last, your task is to make it hard for your opponent to say no to you. In other words, you can educate your opponent about the consequences of a failure to reach agreement. One way of educating is to ask thought-provoking questions, such as, "What do you think will happen if we don't agree?"

Mike told Larry that if they didn't reach some agreement, Mike's parents might decide to press charges against Larry. Mike said he didn't want that to happen; it would only deepen the hostility.

At this point, having others on your side can really help. You may need someone to monitor a permanent agreement. (Mike and Andy used a teacher and the counselor.) The goal is for you and your opponent to feel mutually satisfied.

Mike complimented Larry on his strength and athletic ability. He invited Larry to a "lock-up" party at his church the following Friday night. The youth group planned to order pizza and have various athletic contests at which Mike knew Larry would excel.

During the negotiations that followed, the counselor told Larry he would not report the pushing incident to Larry's parents if Larry agreed to go to the party. Larry agreed.

At the end of the meeting, the counselor took Mike and Andy aside. He told them that, if necessary, they could have passes to leave school five minutes early each day. Or the two could wait a few minutes after school in the counselor's office. If the incidents continued, Mike and Andy could come back to the counselor and ask for help.

The negotiations did not make Larry and Mike become best friends. Larry did go to the party, however, and had a great time. He won a cake for lifting the heaviest weights. Larry even joined the church youth group. Most important, he began to feel better about his own unique talents and left Mike and Andy alone.

PUPPIES WHO HURT

Remember, those who cause bias incidents are people with problems. They are "hurting puppies." They are frustrated, angry, and scared. They feel misunderstood and ignored.

We have already discussed some of the reasons people commit bias incidents. Let's see what sometimes happens to the chronic victims of bias. People who constantly hear that they are worthless feel worthless. People who are treated like dirt feel like dirt. These people hurt. They develop ways of dealing with their pain. Some of these reactions are useful; some are not. What are some of these responses?

Anxiety

One trait of the chronic victim is anxiety. How would you behave if you were not sure you'd be welcome when you entered a public place or a private home? Because of constant strain, chronic victims of bias may seem angry at the world. If they are unable to express their anger in socially acceptable ways, they may vent it in unacceptable ways.

Noah, seventeen

"A black kid in my class painted swastikas on Jewish people's sidewalks. I once heard him say he hated racism. He sure picked a strange way to show it. I can't understand why he did that. After all, he's a minority too. He should know how a minority person feels."

Dan, fourteen

"I was at the mall with another Jewish friend. While we were waiting for our ride, this guy put his hand in the air and saluted like Hitler. I turned away, but a few minutes later he came up to us and did the same thing again. I told him Hitler would have killed him because Hitler wanted a pure white race, and the guy who tormented us was Hispanic."

Denial

Remember the New Testament story in which Jesus predicted that his follower Peter would deny him three times? Victims of bias may deny membership in their group to be better able to get along in the larger world.

Tony, seventeen

"Because I look white and not Hispanic, I was able to get into a private party of all Anglos. I was glad to be able to party with my friends, but I didn't feel comfortable about the circumstances. It was only because of the way I looked."

Group Loyalty

Minority group members may cope with discrimination by becoming intensely loyal to their own group, showing prejudice to other groups, or fighting back. In the example below, a high school sophomore stands up for her racial group.

Meg, fifteen

"It hurts me more than anything when people judge me on the basis of my color instead of my personality. Every day I'm surrounded by people who hate blacks, who think they're better than us because their skin color is white. Personally I'm proud to be black. No one can or ever will change that. I just wish white people would accept me instead of shunning me."

Sandy and Mary Jane, seventeen

These two young women work at Wendy's, sometimes on the same shift. They also go to the same school and are in some of the same classes. While at work, they are good friends. They joke around with the customers and with each other. At the restaurant, Sandy is one of a few black employees; on occasion she has felt left out.

The school's racial mix is approximately half white and half black. Mary Jane sometimes feels hurt when Sandy gets together with her black friends and acts as if she and Mary Jane had never met.

One day they both attended a senior prom decorating committee meeting at which Mary Jane was the only white girl. Sandy, involved in conversation with a black friend, totally ignored Mary Jane. For once, thought Sandy, I feel comfortable. Although Sandy often felt excluded at work, it didn't occur to her that Mary Jane would ever have similar feelings.

If Mary Jane could put herself in Sandy's place at work, she would be sure to include Sandy in after-work activities. Perhaps one of the girls should "break the ice" and share her feelings with the other.

Examples of group loyalty abound. A newspaper columnist criticized black leader Jesse Jackson for not taking a stand against the violence and racism of rap music lyrics. Instead, Jackson criticized President (then candidate) Bill Clinton for criticizing them. The columnist was upset that a black leader would be so careful not to show disloyalty to his own group.

As in the example below, women often develop an intense loyalty to the sisterhood of women.

Ella, fifteen

"I believe that everyone no matter what race, religion, sex, or otherwise has been subjected to bias at one time or another. As a woman, I am part of the largest group of people discriminated against and possibly one of the most forgotten groups. Many other groups' needs are dealt with, but women do not get their fair share."

Amy, eighteen

"I'm walking down the hall, minding my own business, and these black girls call me names, such as "white ---,' or 'snob,' or -----.' I know I'm none of these, so I feel it's unprovoked. It has happened to me many times. Some of my friends have had incidents in which black girls started fights with them for no reason."

If Amy could understand that the black girls in question are dealing with their pain by "fighting back," she might be better able to tolerate their attacks.

Self-Hate

An unfortunate result of minority group oppression is self-hate. Some people begin to believe what they hear about themselves and internalize this negative picture of themselves. The doll experiment described in Chapter 1 is an example. Black children who chose white dolls changed their minds after researchers pointed out the desirable characteristics of the black dolls.

In another example, a group of African-American young people in a restaurant got into an argument about money. The astonished diners heard these shouts from the black youngsters themselves: "Hey, nigger. Get away from me, nigger. Stop it, you ugly black nigger!"

Self-hate may become so intense that it flares into violence. Gang members often prey on their own cultural and ethnic group because of self-hatred and low self-esteem.

Why Me?

The search for reasons is often a major task for victims of bias incidents. Likewise, a person who has watched another person suffer from bias may have questions.

Amber, fourteen

Amber is Anglo. In seventh and eighth grades she attended a "mostly Hispanic" school. This arrangement worked out well "most of the time." In eighth grade Amber and another girl were the only whites on the basketball team. At one game, spectators pointed at them, booed them, and laughed at their mistakes. Suddenly Amber and her friend felt like bad guys.

In trying to make sense of things, Amber asked herself, Why am I the color I am? She felt angry at her "whiteness." Finally she tried to see the situation in a different light. She understood for the first time how those of any minority must feel most of the time. She felt good about her new insight.

Guilt and Shame

Outsiders may see victims as losers. They may think that the victim did something to provoke the incident. Unfortunately, victims themselves may develop feelings of shame and guilt.

Khoa, fifteen

Khoa's parents became citizens of the United States before his birth; he was born in Wisconsin. In eighth grade, a group of boys surrounded him chanting racial slurs. Two of them began to hit him. Somehow Khoa pushed himself out of the circle and ran home. He never saw the boys again. Later, however, he discovered in himself feelings of shame about his Vietnamese heritage.

Eleanor, fifty-three

Eleanor is the mother of four young-adult children. She is also a high school English teacher. Both of her parents were born in Germany and spoke German as well as English in their Minnesota home. They taught Ellie German poems and songs. Not under-standing the world situation at the time (the Hitler era), Ellie went forth into the community and sang her German songs. She recalls running home in tears when older kids called her a "Nazi." Her parents abruptly stopped the language lessons, and Ellie began to be ashamed of her German heritage. Many years later she understood the situation, but she still wishes she could speak German.

ACCENTUATING THE POSITIVE

Lest we get mired in the swamp of negativity, let's move on to some useful and productive ways of coping with bias incidents. Several healthy coping techniques are: (1) trying harder, (2) using healthy anger, (3) asserting your-self, (4) having high self-esteem, and (5) developing non-violent skills.

TRYING HARDER

As Errol Smith says in 37 *Things Every Black Man Needs to Know*, "Don't get mad; get motivated—then get busy!" The following incidents have to do with being short. Because contemporary society tends to devalue short people, all three young people fought back by trying harder.

Carmen, fifteen

I'm a dwarf and as a result have many orthopedic problems. A band teacher once told me that I shouldn't take up the saxophone because my handicap wouldn't allow me to play it well, if at all. He assumed that I was incapable of playing the instrument, and maybe that I wasn't even remotely intelligent. The whole thing made me so angry, I not only learned to play the saxophone but went on to make first chair in all-city orchestra. Since then, I've also learned to play the clarinet, oboe, and piano. I guess I wanted to prove the band teacher wrong. Afterward I felt much better about myself—that I was not as limited as they or I had previously thought."

Ted, fourteen

"It was in soccer. I'm much smaller than most of the guys, so they thought they could push me around. But I played more aggressively and worked harder than anyone else to get better at the game. When I played hard against them, they played hard against me. Trying harder made me feel like a huge person."

Heather, fourteen

"I'm not short; I'm 'vertically challenged.' At four feet, ten inches I'm used to being the smallest person in my class. I don't plan to let my height set me back in life. Many people 'reach for the stars,' and I am going to reach as far as I have to, even if for me it's a little more of a stretch."

USING HEALTHY ANGER

Robert Guillaume

Guillaume, born in 1927, was raised by his grandmother, who made him feel special and loved. According to an article in *PARADE* magazine (May 24, 1992), his teachers praised him for his intelligence as well as for his singing ability. When he was about ten, however, he began to hear the undercurrent of negative messages that poor black children receive in this society. In essence he heard that he was inferior, dumb, and would never amount to anything. These messages made Guillaume angry; he knew he was smart, and he couldn't figure out what color had to do with anything. His anger kept his confidence alive. When he considers the biased treatment of African-Americans to this day, he still feels angry. But Guillaume used his anger well. He went to college, studied singing, auditioned for parts in Broadway productions, and experienced rejection.

Angry at the system, he adopted an I-don't-care-what-you-think attitude. He decided, however, to prove that blacks could make it in theater. He began to succeed. Ultimately he won a Tony Award nomination, his own TV series, two Emmy Awards, and the lead in the Los Angeles production of "Phantom of the Opera." As Guillaume looks back on his life, he finds that the secret is not to avoid anger but to focus it in order to generate creative energy from it.

Healthy anger can motivate us to make changes in ourselves, in others, and in the world, but getting furious at people and calling them names does no good. What counts is *action*. Robert Guillaume took action. He kept trying. In the meantime, he improved himself. When he failed, he tried again. Eventually he succeeded "big time" in his chosen field.

Although anger that explodes can be harmful, so can anger that is "swallowed." Many of us learned as little children *not* to get angry. When we showed anger, our parents or other adults got angry at *us*. Therefore, we learned to swallow our anger and not to express it. Swallowed anger can make people sick. Headaches, stomachaches, ulcers, and addictions may result.

In many of the examples we've seen so far, people subjected to bias incidents became angry. Most, however, did not know what to do with their anger. Some were too angry at the time of the incident to do anything but leave the scene. Let's review several of the stories from Chapter 3.

In Brian's story, a clerk stood on the counter to make sure Brian and his friends didn't steal anything. Brian was angry and insulted at the clerk's actions. He left the store, which was not the worst thing he could have done. But he wondered what else he could have done.

He *could* have explained his feelings to the clerk. In response, the clerk might have told Brian how much money his boss had lost to shoplifters. Maybe nothing would have changed. On the other hand, Brian might have felt better after expressing his views. He and his friends also might have felt empathy for the clerk and for the store manager who had lost money.

In Marcia's story, a boy shouted racial slurs at her when she refused to give him her basketball. In return, she did the same thing to him. What could she have done? She might have confronted the boy and demanded that he treat her with respect. She might have said, "I'm Marcia.

If you'd like to use my name, I'd be glad to share my basketball with you. What's your name?"

In another incident, eighth-grade boys called Marcia's friend Natasha racial names. Natasha told her teacher, who then told the principal, who got the attackers to apologize to Natasha.

What you might do when confronted with similar incidents depends on the circumstances. It may even depend on your mood at the time. As mentioned earlier, many who reported harassment made sure not to react immediately after an incident. A cooling-off period of minutes or hours can be very helpful.

After a cooling-off period, you may be ready to confront the person who made you angry. Certain skills can make this confrontation work to your advantage. First, be positive. When you speak, find something good to start with. In the following situation, Liz, our computer expert, thought that Stuart was hogging the computer they shared.

> Liz: "It's fun working with you, Stuart. I enjoy being your partner, but when I see someone bent over a keyboard for hours, I worry about that person's back. Also, I wonder if I'll ever be asked if *I* have some work to do. Sometimes I feel angry."

Second, express your anger using "I" messages. Liz said "*I* feel angry" rather than, "You make me angry." To keep the other person from becoming defensive, try to keep the "you" out of your message. Examples of "I" messages are: "When I am called a racial name, I see red." Or, "When someone stereotypes me, I feel put down." Practice "I" messages until they come easily and naturally.

Third, stick to the point. Don't drag in ancient or modern history even if it seems relevant. In the heat of the moment, your opponent does not want to hear something like this: "I called you a name because I'm African-American, and I am angry that the United States let a boat full of people from Haiti drown because they were black." Or, "As a Native American, I have a right to smash windshields of cars belonging to the Anglos who took our land away from us." Such angry outbursts are not conducive to building the bridges to reconciliation that most of us would like to build.

ASSERTING YOURSELF

What's the difference between assertiveness and aggressiveness? Being aggressive may step on another person's toes and cause hurt. Being assertive is standing up for yourself and your rights. No one likes being a doormat, but sometimes we do allow other people to step on us. How do we keep this from happening?

In the first place, be firm. Don't start out by apologizing for living. In other words, don't say something like this: "Excuse me, I'm sorry to bother you, but I wonder if you realize that you're sitting at my desk?"

Again, use "I" messages. Tell the person how his behavior makes you feel. For example: "I can't get my work done with you at my desk."

Third, stick to the subject. Be clear about what you want: "In the next three seconds I want you to remove your stuff from my desk."

Fourth, tell the person what will happen if the desired behavior does not occur. Try to be positive about the good that could happen. "If you don't move, I'll report you to the monitor. Perhaps he can find you a permanent desk."

You can apply the same techniques in dealing with bias incidents. Take Anna from Chapter 1. A longtime "friend" (Jack) said he hated blondes. Anna waited until later to confront him, but she could have talked to Jack the minute he spoke. The following are some ways—one wrong and three right—to deal with such remarks.

Jack: "I *hate* blondes. They're all stupid."

Anna: (wrong way) "Well, I hate to mention it, but I guess you didn't notice my hair color."

Anna: (better way) "I have a hard time understanding what a person's hair color has to do with his or her intelligence."

Jack: "I would never date a blonde. They're dumb."

Anna: (telling how she feels) "In case you didn't notice, I'm a blonde, and your joke doesn't make me feel like laughing."

Jack: (smiling) "I would never date a blonde. They're all idiots."

Anna: (smiling too) "I don't have time for stereotypes. (Gets up.) There's my friend Damien. I'm going to go talk to him. If you have something more intelligent to say later, maybe we can get together."

HAVING HIGH SELF-ESTEEM

We all know it's important to love ourselves. Why? For one reason, we can't love anyone else until we do. For another, others will love us only to the extent that we care about ourselves. We have already seen that the people who put others down and cause bias incidents are those who have little or no self-respect. On the other hand, many people go through life behaving like victims. When they take the bull by the horns and assume control over their lives, they begin to feel much better about themselves. Jawanza Kunjufu, author of numerous books on the black condition, says that racism is a sign of insecurity. When people feel secure, they are comfortable with differences.

In an entertaining book called *Making Friends: A Guide to Getting Along with People*, Andrew Matthews asks, "How can I feel good about me?" He suggests several things you can do. First, stop comparing yourself unfavorably to others. Second, set meaningful, achievable goals for yourself. Make a list of all the kind and caring things you've done in the past week. Finally, don't expect someone else to come along and make you happy. Make *yourself* happy, and people will be attracted to you.

Anyone who has ever had to cope with bias is likely to feel like a victim. Dr. Julius Segal, author of *Winning Life's Toughest Battles*, suggests five "Cs" that will help anyone who has ever felt like a victim come out a winner.

The first "C" is communication. If you are the victim of a bias incident, find someone to talk to. The person you choose could be a friend, a parent, or someone at school, such as a teacher or counselor.

Talking about what happened will make you feel better. Also, some unexpected changes may result. Jennifer chose to talk to some people she hoped would be able to do something about the incident.

Jennifer, seventeen

Jennifer is an Anglo-American senior at a racially integrated school. In her sophomore year she tried out for cheerleading. When the cheerleaders already on the squad added up the points, some of the blacks and some of the whites were chosen. But when the football coach, the only adult judge, announced *his* results, only the black students (all the black students who had tried out) had made the squad.

Jennifer got together the current cheerleaders, the newly chosen cheerleaders, and those who had not made the cut. They all agreed to take the matter to the principal. After hearing what had happened, the principal put all those who had tried out on the squad.

Jennifer learned that any person can harbor prejudice, even a faculty member who should know better. She was angry that the coach was not disciplined for his biased behavior , but she learned that life is sometimes unfair. At least Jennifer exercised her option of communication and got results.

Although you may blame someone else for the incident itself, take responsibility for your own *feelings* about what happened. Let's stress the "I" message again. Don't say, "He made me mad." Instead say, "I was angry when the coach acted in a biased way." An "I" message gives you, the speaker, a feeling of control. *You* are the one who chooses to get angry. Remember: You do have choices.

Ultimately Jennifer exercised another choice: She chose to quit cheerleading. The next year, however, the principal named an integrated group of faculty members to do the judging.

A racial attack or bias incident may leave the victim almost speechless. Only by expressing your feelings in a controlled manner, however, will you be able to preserve your dignity.

In the meeting with the principal, Jennifer used some ideas she had learned in a class on conflict resolution. She was able to state the problem clearly because she realized that both parties had something to gain in successful solution of the situation. In the negotiations, Jennifer and her friends of various races learned a great deal about the challenges the principal faced in running the school. He in turn left the meeting with a greater appreciation of the students and the challenges *they* faced.

The second "C" is to take control. Unfortunately, by its very nature a bias incident may make you feel totally out of control. Nevertheless you must find a way to stay in charge.

Psychologists Hopson and Hopson, who did the experiment with the black and white dolls, report that a group of young black men utilized the following ways of coping with being black in a racist society.

- They thought through their actions on their own and did not blindly follow others.
- They took pride in themselves.
- They resisted negative peer pressure.
- They remembered the lessons their parents had taught them.
- They communicated with their parents.

Kunjufu suggests that young black males:

- Learn about and appreciate their culture, including its history.

- Develop their talents, not only in sports and music but also in reading, writing, and computer skills.
- Learn how to earn and handle money.
- Learn time management skills.
- Stay away from nicotine, caffeine, and drugs.
- Develop a relationship with God.
- Learn that racism is a sign of insecurity.

In this way, he says, black males will be able to develop their full potential. Actually any young person would do well to follow this advice.

The third "C" is conviction. Conviction means trying to find a reason for what has happened. Each of us looks for meaning in life. After a bias incident, you may feel that life is meaningless or without purpose.

Jennifer found greater meaning in the conflict resolution process. The issue was not only which person of what race would make up the cheerleading squad. The issue, she thought, was a larger one. Because the school had a diverse ethnic mix, Jennifer thought the cheerleaders should represent that diversity. Furthermore, they should be able to show others in the school, as well as in society at large, that a multiracial group could get along. In the process of conflict resolution, the group did pull together and gained a satisfactory outcome to their problem.

Fourth, have a clear conscience. Be sure actions on your part were not the cause of a bias incident. A victim who feels guilty is likely to withdraw from the help others may offer.

Theresa, fourteen

"Both of my grandparents came from Italy, and I have dark curly hair. When I was in sixth grade, I went to Sunday School with my best friend. We sat in a circle, and some boys on the other side of the room started giggling and whispering and pointing at me. They said cruel words like "greasy Italian" and "Mafia Mama,"and they asked me if I ate spaghetti for breakfast. I felt ashamed of my Italian name. I felt dirty and embarrassed about who I was. It seemed that everyone was staring at me. The incident hurt my heart."

Theresa would be the first to agree with professionals who observe that hate crimes and bias incidents often make their victims feel fearful, left out, and disliked. In spite of knowing that the problem existed outside herself, Theresa let the prejudices of others make her feel terrible.

The final "C" is compassion. Wrapped up in your own self-concern and self-pity, you may fail to do what would help the most in your healing process: help others.

Pam, fifteen

"I went to a public school in the core city. Kids used to make fun of my Polish name. They also made fun of me because I was white. (The school was 95 percent black.) I was beaten up and picked on, and I had few friends. What made things worse was that I had a biased teacher (also black). At first I tried to ignore everything that happened, but that didn't help. Then I talked to people about it—parents, teachers, school board members. As I got older, I learned how to deal with the daily problems, and I improved my self-defense. I talked directly and privately to the people who caused problems.

This one guy I talked to didn't have many friends either because he was kind of big and nerdy. When he found out that I was a nice person, we became friends, and he helped defend me. By being his friend, I helped him too. Eventually I became stronger and more independent."

DEVELOPING NONVIOLENT SKILLS

According to Terrence Webster-Doyle, author of *Why Is Everybody Always Picking on Me? A Guide to Handling Bullies*, nonviolent skills include self-defense skills such as karate and other alternatives to conflict.

Karate builds confidence. The skills you can learn from a qualified teacher of martial arts include blocking, punching, kicking, and striking. Rather than tensing up, running away, or reacting in anger, you can learn to become "centered." The best part of having karate skills under your "belt" is that you may be able to scare off your attacker before you have take action. Find an instructor who will teach you both the physical and the mental skills of self-defense.

The following are nonviolent ways of coping with bias incidents. See if you can think of others.

Ignoring, Walking Away, or Refusing to Fight

It takes at least two to start a fight. If you refuse to fight by ignoring the aggressor or by walking away, he can't start anything.

Roman, eighteen

"Because I'm tall and black, the cops (especially the white cops) are always following me around. In a store, one cop walked about two feet behind me. I pretended he wasn't there and went about my business."

Agreeing (or Respectfully Disagreeing)

Strange as it seems, one good way of defusing the anger that you feel in the midst of a bias incident (or afterward) is to agree with your attacker. "Wait a minute," you say, "if someone calls me a nerd, am I supposed to agree?" Not in so many words, perhaps, but you could say something like this: "So you think I'm smart? Well, I am, so I'm not sure I want to talk to you." Say whatever you decide to say with a smile. Who knows, maybe the rude person will smile back.

If you're not in the mood to agree with someone who calls you names, you can disagree in a nonviolent, nonthreatening way. Remember that your goal is to prevent a fight, stop the abusive cycle, and preserve your dignity. Say someone calls you one of the names you've heard all too many times—"nigger" or "monkey," for example. A dignified response would be to reply quietly, "I'm African-American (or Afro-American), and I'd appreciate receiving the respect I deserve."

Cal, sixteen

"I was the victim of a bias incident because of my age. I was trying to exchange a shirt I'd gotten for Christmas. It had the original tags on it, and I had the sales slip. When I went into the store to make the exchange, the saleswoman gave me the runaround. I left with the shirt under my arm. My mom took it in the next day and exchanged it—no questions asked. An hour after Mom came home, I went back to the store and found the clerk who had jerked me around. I talked to her calmly and respectfully for about fifteen minutes. She finally apologized, and I felt better."

Standing Up for Yourself

The opposite of walking away is (obviously) to stand up to those who threaten you. Your response may surprise them and make them back off.

Wendy, seventeen

"I'm Hispanic and white mixed, and these Hispanic girls were picking on me because I wasn't like them. I didn't dress like them or comb my hair the way they did. They called me 'little white girl.' I stuck up for myself, and others stuck up for me also. I told them I was still like them; I just enjoyed different activities. Finally the girls grew out of it and let me alone. I was glad I stood up to them. I felt confident in who I was."

Using Humor

Lightening the mood may be one way to defuse tensions following a bias incident. Be careful, though, that the person you're responding to doesn't think you're making fun of him or her.

Heather, the short person quoted earlier, hates being called "short stuff," "shortie," or "shrimp." She feels like strangling the person speaking. Instead she chooses a response to lighten things up. "Hey, good things come in small packages." Or, "The tall have farther to fall."

Getting Help

When you are involved in a bias incident, getting help from an adult is not a sign of weakness but a sign of strength and intelligence. Natasha's problem involved name-calling. Natasha told a teacher, who told the principal. Natasha felt better when the principal insisted that the boys who called her names apologize to her.

Role Playing/Rehearsing

"Sure, sure," you say, "I already know all those coping techniques, but when someone calls me names I forget everything I've learned. What I want to do is to lash out and hurt someone."

One way to say what you want to say rather than the angry words that leap to mind is to practice your responses ahead of time. This rehearsing is often called "role playing."

Ian, sixteen

Ian knows that when he goes to the speech meet at least one person is going to make a hurtful remark about his private school. Parker Academy is a special school for young people with learning disabilities. Before Ian started there, he could not have stood before a crowd, much less make a speech. Ian anticipates a bias incident and practices his responses ahead of time.

Here are some further examples of defusing, discussed in Chapter 4.

Tormentor:	"Why do you go to a snobby academy? Are your parents rich?"
Possible response #1:	"I wish they were. I could use some cash. Do you have any?"
Possible response #2:	"Why do you ask? Do you need a loan?"
Possible response #3:	"No, they're not. I'm on scholarship because I'm smart."

April, fifteen

April is auditioning for a part in a play. From past experience she knows someone will remark about her short stature. She wants to be ready, so she practices her responses to possible comments.

Tormentor:	"You're in high school? What happened? Did you drink too much coffee?"
Possible response:	"Don't you know you can't tell the depth of the well by the size of the pump handle."

THE VICTORY OF RECOVERY

Morton Bard and Dawn Sangrey, authors of *The Crime Victim's Book*, tell us that the victim's ultimate victory is a good recovery. When a crime victim comes out of the

crisis with strength renewed, he or she has triumphed.
We can say the same about victims of bias incidents.
Many high school students report a similar pride in
triumph over prejudice.

Rosalie, fifteen

Two years ago Rosalie came from Mexico to Texas
with her parents. Not long afterward, her parents
moved within the state, and she had to start over
again in a new school. A teacher she barely knew
singled her out for "unpleasant looks, nasty remarks,
and rude comments." A few days after these encounters, a friend asked Rosalie if she would get his
notebook out of his locker for him. The same teacher
came up behind Rosalie, told her she had no
business there, and laughed. Afterward, Rosalie
could still feel the teacher's breath on her neck. She
went into the girls' bathroom and cried. Later she
missed an important exam. She remembers feeling
"tortured." She felt as if she had nowhere to go with
her grief.

For a long time after this incident, Rosalie felt "not
good enough." Normally she's an active young
person who goes to church, belongs to school clubs,
does volunteer work, plays tennis, rides her bike,
does homework, goes out with friends, and enjoys
spending time with her parents. Now she felt like
quitting everything. She still feels like running
whenever she sees that teacher.

Rosalie kept going to school, but she made an effort to
avoid the teacher who had verbally abused her. In some
ways it made her feel better to learn that the teacher had

treated others the same way. In some ways it made her feel worse. After all, this woman was a teacher. Finally Rosalie decided not to let one person ruin her life. "I picked myself up," she said, "and kept on living."

Christopher, eighteen

Christopher experienced a kind of prejudice that gave him an understanding of what others put up with—sometimes for their whole lives. Chris is white but lives in a part of town that is primarily Hispanic. When he sent his résumé for a job as a receptionist, he received a reply by return mail: The company did not hire Mexican gang members. Chris took the letter to the company's office and demanded to see the person in charge of personnel. While the personnel director stared, Chris showed him the letter and his picture identification. He said that even if he were offered a job, he would never work for a company that rated people by the location of their homes. Afterward Chris said, "I wanted to cuss at him, but I didn't because it would have showed I was no better than he was."

Chris's story illustrates one person's understanding of the world as an imperfect place. Chris was proud of his ability to rise above the tactics of a company that treated an entire group of people without respect. No one would disagree, however, that such incidents can leave the recipient with invisible scars.

Trina, fifteen

Trina loves volleyball and tennis, movies and books. "I'm an active person," she says with a smile, "but I

have a very big nose. All my life I've been pushed
out by certain people because of my appearance.
There's nothing I can do about it, except maybe have
surgery. But I'm having second thoughts on that. If
my friends can't accept me for who I am, they aren't
true friends."

As Trina has grown older, she has come to believe
that most of the people in her circle do accept her
and even consider her pretty because of her inner
qualities. But when someone makes a cruel or
insensitive remark, Trina still hurts. On occasion she
has felt, "I'm a nothing or a nobody. I feel as if I have
a broken heart."

Cox News Service reporter Elizabeth Coady reports
that 644,000 cosmetic surgery procedures were performed
in the United States in 1990, a 69 percent increase over
1991. Three percent or close to twenty thousand of these
surgeries were performed on children under eighteen.
Many people decry the American obsession with "beauty"
and physical perfection. According to Coady's news story,
Robert Mashman, a California psychologist who special-
izes in the psychological effects of changed appearance,
does not approve of the trend. He considers it risky to
base self-esteem on appearances.

Anyone who has spent five minutes with Trina can tell
that she's a valuable person, someone who makes others
feel good about themselves. Dealing with her "handicap"
has given her an inner strength. "It's what's inside that
counts," says Trina. "Beauty is only skin-deep."

Randy, fifteen

Randy is of Japanese-American ancestry. He plays
soccer, swims, and participates in drama at school.

One bias incident sticks out in his mind. He got into an argument with Frank, a guy he calls a "loser." Nevertheless Frank's words, "Get back on the tuna boat where you belong," hurt. Randy, who has lots of friends, told them about the incident. From that time on, he and his friends considered Frank a racist and stayed away from him.

Camille, fourteen

Camille is biracial (black/white). Like most ninth graders, she wants very much to "fit in." One memorable day, however, a group of black girls told her to "act her color," and a group of white girls accused her of having a "black attitude."

Camille was confused, hurt, and angry. She didn't know where she fit in or if she fit in at all. Luckily she has understanding and caring parents, who helped her refine her philosophy of life. "I learned that people will think what they want to think. Their attitudes don't stop me from pursuing my goals." From then on, Camille was better able to put her life and identity in perspective.

COPING WHEN YOU ARE NOT THE TARGET

At one time or another, almost everyone experiences prejudice of some kind. Therefore, almost everyone is sympathetic with the victim. Not only the victim, however, but also the onlooker may feel a sense of help-lessness and hopelessness.

Doug, fifteen

"I was walking down the hall with my friend. A white teacher kept asking all the black kids for a pass. My friend and I, both white, walked right past her. In fact, we looked her in the eye. Still she didn't ask us for a pass. (We didn't have one.) I was astonished and also angry to think that a grown-up would treat a group of people that way."

Even if you feel helpless, there are things you can do. In fact, you *should* do something, not only to make yourself feel in control but also to help end the cycle of bias and violence.

What are some of those things? First, become secure about your own identity, the person you are. Work on having high self-esteem so that you won't let bias get you down. Then you won't have to retaliate by putting others down.

Second, appreciate the differences in people; diversity makes life interesting. Make it a point to associate with people who are different from you in some way and learn whatever you can from them. Try to plan and participate in activities that will bring people of different cultures together.

Eric, twenty-one

Eric entered college at the age when most of his friends had already graduated. He chose a small private school in North Dakota, where he found the winters long and harsh. He felt "too old" for some of the activities that went on in the dorm. In searching for ways to pass the time on Sundays, Eric hit upon an idea that brought people together. As a person who loved to eat, he decided to organize Sunday evening "ethnic suppers." Eric found students from India, Japan, Mexico, and Ethiopia who were willing to mastermind the preparation of their country's cuisine. He even persuaded the school's kitchen to provide the ingredients. The cultural evenings expanded to include native dances and games. Eric's dinners drew students from all over the campus for a night of fun and cultural education.

A third way of coping with bias incidents directed at others is to refuse to stand by. According to Margaret Thatcher, former Prime Minister of Great Britain, "Standing in the middle of the road is very dangerous; you get knocked down by traffic from both sides." Elie Wiesel, the author mentioned in Chapter 1, says, "Take sides. Neutrality helps the oppressor, never the victim. Silence encourages the tormentor, never the tormented." Don't tolerate bias incidents if there's anything you can do to stop them. Armed with a knowledge of prejudice, you can educate others.

Report hate crimes to parents, teachers, and the police. Be sure of your facts; as soon as possible after the incident, write down the details. Call the National Hate Hotline, 1-800-347-HATE, or the National Organization for Victim Assistance, 1-202-232-6682. In addition, you can contact any of the organizations listed in the Appendix.

LISTENING: WHAT NOT TO DO

You can help victims of bias incidents by being a good listener. Your friend will need to talk and will undoubtedly feel more comfortable talking to you than to an adult. Most of us need some reminders about how to be a good listener. Mary Lynne Heldman, author of *When Words Hurt*, offers some advice on what *not* to do. The following are a few of the many roadblocks to effective listening.

- *Interrupting.* How often do you jump in, unable to hold back your comments until the speaker has finished?
- *Advice-giving/Lecturing/Directing.* Telling the speaker what she *should* do is usually not the response she wants from you.
- *Warning/Threatening.* Predicting a dire outcome may turn the person totally off.
- *Interpreting.* "I think what you really mean is . . ." sounds as if you are playing psychologist.
- *Identifying.* "That reminds me of an incident I had not too long ago." Your friend doesn't want to hear what happened to you; he wants to tell what happened to *him.*
- *Criticizing.* Even though what you say may be true, the speaker is already feeling vulnerable and is in no mood for put-downs.

Heldman points out that a good listener may use some of these techniques, but only at the proper time. That time is when the speaker has finished talking and is ready to hear what you have to say.

LISTENING: WHAT TO DO

We know what *not* to do, but what can we *do* to become good listeners? The first thing to do is to be quiet. If you need a piece of masking tape over your lips to keep you silent, bring on the tape.

Second, make sure the speaker knows you are listening. Give your undivided attention. Show your interest by eye contact, alertness, nodding once in a while.

Third, repeat back what you are hearing. If you're not sure you heard correctly, you can ask questions, but be sure to phrase them in a noncritical, nonjudgmental way.

Finally, use "reflective listening." This technique is easy and effective. By listening to the *feelings* underlying the words, you can often zero in on the real problem and help the speaker realize that, for a change, someone is hearing him.

Lynn and Marge

Lynn, fourteen, comes home from school and says, "I hate this neighborhood. When can we move?" In response, her sister Marge, eighteen, might have said, "Never. Mom and Dad have always said they want to die in this house." Marge would have missed a chance to hear what was really on Lynn's mind. Instead Marge said, "You sound pretty upset. Did something happen on the way home from school?" Lynn could hardly wait to blurt out her story. On the bus, a boy she hated had called her "Chubs." Lynn talked for ten minutes about the "geek" who had made her life miserable ever since fifth grade. The sisters ended up having a good laugh over shared memories. As a result of having been listened to, Lynn had a productive evening with some difficult homework; Marge felt good about having helped her sister.

In addition to being a good listener, you can become a peacemaker or conflict manager. Sometimes all that is needed in a disagreement is a neutral or objective person who can listen to both sides and make suggestions for change.

Kate Benton, sixteen, gave up her lunch hours to act as a peer counselor at her high school. A listener as well as a conflict manager, she made several new friends from various racial and ethnic groups.

STRESSING OUT

Having to cope with bias incidents when you are the target is bound to cause stress. Even if you are only a witness to a bias incident, stress may result.

Remember Carolyn, who witnessed the bias incident on Martin Luther King Day? Carolyn's anger at the situation caused her breathing rate and pulse rate to increase. At one point in the aftermath of the demonstration, she felt as if she might faint right in the middle of the sidewalk.

Other short-term effects of stress are nausea, headaches, a sense of anxiety, such as pin-pricks all over the body, or a sense of impending doom. Long-term effects may be weight gain or loss, fatigue, depression, addictions, and various illnesses such as stomach ulcers.

In "Calming Jangled Nerves" (*Better Homes and Gardens*, August 1992), Nick Gallo writes that you can't always change stressful situations immediately. You can, however, change the way you respond to them.

One way to take charge is at least to try to bring about change. Setting meaningful goals is another take-charge strategy. Stay open-minded. Realize that your actions often do bring about results. Get rid of negative thoughts; never say "never."

Although Gallo suggests concentrating on trying to change what you *can* change, some situations may not respond to your efforts. In these cases you will have to make an attitude adjustment.

In Chapter 4, Traci, an African-American student, found that white peers in her advanced-placement English class avoided her. While she couldn't change the way her classmates responded to her, she could take a philosophical look at her situation. She told herself that she was getting the same education her classmates were getting, she had plenty of friends, and she had a prosperous and loving family.

Jessica, sixteen

Jessica, an Anglo-American, is the older of two girls in the Snelling family. Her sister, Amanda, is fourteen. In addition to the girls and their parents, the family includes two foster children. These siblings, James and Richard, are biracial (black/white). The Snelling family has developed a loving attachment to James and Richard and would like to adopt them. The agency would like to find a black or biracial family for the boys, but the caseworker worries about disrupting their attachment to the foster family. The caseworker also worries about an Anglo family's ability to meet the boys' racial identity needs. One day when Jessica was putting James on the bus for preschool, two white teenagers stopped their car behind the school bus. "Hey," yelled the driver, "get that little nigger out of the street." "Wait a minute," Jessica yelled back, "he's half white." Jessica was proud of herself for defending her foster brother. But when she told the incident to the boys' caseworker that afternoon, the caseworker pointed out Jessica's mistake. In her effort to be supportive of James, she had ended up apologizing for the part of him that was black.

As a result of the incident and the caseworker's criticism, Jessica felt stressed. But she said to herself: "I can't change the racist attitudes of those guys. I can't change the fact that I'm white and my little brothers are biracial. I can't change society right this minute. I can't change what I said, but I can learn from this incident. I did the best I could at the time. Next time I'll try to do better."

Get Busy!

Being too busy can create stress. But as a general rule, getting involved, getting busy, relieves stress. What works varies from person to person. Some people like to meditate, some like to read or sing, some enjoy writing in a journal, some take a warm bath or shower. Some people like to volunteer to help others. Any kind of exercise is likely to relieve stress. Try walking, running, roller-blading, swimming, playing tennis, or playing golf. How about dancing, weight lifting, aerobics, basketball, or yoga? Or try a combination of the above. Most of all, have fun!

Organizations devoted to the relief of stress are the American Institute of Stress, 124 Park Avenue, Department B, Yonkers, NY 10703, and the Hardiness Institute, 19742 MacArthur Boulevard, Suite 100, Irvine, CA 92715.

Posttraumatic Stress Disorder

This mental disturbance sometimes affects persons who have experienced or witnessed violence. The symptoms may include uncontrollable crying or shaking, nightmares, chronic depression, anxiety attacks, or inability to concentrate, eat, or sleep. Posttrauma symptoms depend on the kind and severity of the incident witnessed or experienced and who was involved.

When symptoms are severe and do not disappear after a reasonable time, you may need to see a mental health counselor. Talking over the incident again and again with an understanding person may help. Some people need reassurance that they did not cause the incident and that the danger has passed. Talking about what happened can get thoughts organized and start the healing process. If you can analyze the experience and turn it into a memory, you will be better able to put it into perspective.

Some counselors suggest drawing pictures or writing accounts of what happened. Victims need to know that the emotions they are feeling are perfectly normal under the circumstances.

Help Others; Help Yourself

No one would argue that self-help groups can substitute for professional counseling, but they can be a great supplement. Self-help groups bring together people who share or who have shared similar problems.

Self-help groups are founded on the following principles: (1) You can help yourself by helping others. (2) Those who have experienced a problem are best able to help others with similar problems. (3) You are not part of the problem; you are part of the solution. (4) The group helps to relieve feelings of isolation. (5) Live one day at a time; you can't solve all your problems at once.

The self-help movement has grown to include 500,000 groups in the United States. The National Self-Help Clearinghouse, founded in 1967, can help you access such a group. Write to them at 25 West 43rd Street, Room 620, New York, NY 10036.

Summary

There are many ways of coping with bias incidents. Some responses, such as feelings of anxiety, self-hate or shame, unhealthy anger, and aggressiveness, do not help the situation and may make it worse. More healthy ways of coping are controlled anger, being assertive, having high self-esteem, using humor, getting help, role-playing, and making a coping plan.

CHAPTER ◇ 6

Hope for the

Future

Remember Jean from Chapter 2? As a delegate from her school, Jean attended a national conference on cultural diversity. On the first day of the conference, Jean had an unsettling experience. On her way to meet the teacher-chaperone, she took the elevator. As she stepped inside, a gorgeous, beautifully dressed girl stared at her. Jean's family didn't have a lot of money. Besides, Jean hated to shop, and she always felt as if her clothes looked slightly tacky. She imagined that the other girl scorned her unstylish outfit. She therefore stared straight ahead at the elevator door. Finally the other girl said, "You're from Arizona?" Jean's hand flew to her name badge. She smiled. "Yes. Are you?" The other girl nodded. "I grew up in Tucson, but now I live in Phoenix."

Afterward Jean thought a great deal about this incident. Every time she thought about it, she winced. She had expected unfriendliness; the other girl had offered friendship. Assuming that the other girl felt superior, Jean had taken on an attitude of inferiority, while the other girl had offered mutuality. Jean realized that she had stereotyped *herself.* She looked forward to learning more at this conference.

On the second day, Jean went to a workshop called "Cross-Cultural Conflict Resolution." Settling into a chair and expecting to hear a dull lecture, she yawned and dutifully pulled out her yellow pad.

But the facilitator, Roberto Chené, had a surprise. "First," he said, "we're going to take time to *listen* to each other."

Jean put her pad under her chair and her pen in her pocket.

"With your cooperation," Chené went on, "I'd like us to take time to do an exercise." The student on Jean's right got up and left the room. "I'd like each of you to choose a partner, someone you don't already know." That should be easy, thought Jean, since I don't know anyone here. The man on Jean's left nodded at her. Oh dear, she thought, I don't want to listen to *him*; he looks older than my father. Jean gave half a thought to leaving the room too, but she didn't want to hurt the older man's feelings.

"Now," said Chené, "if we're all settled, I'll explain the rules of the game. For the first five minutes, one of you will be the Listener; the Talker will tell his or her life story. Listeners may not interrupt, interject, or ask questions. Just listen. Okay?"

The participants nodded.

"In five minutes," said Chené, "we'll switch, and the other person will listen."

As the Listener, Jean surprised herself by getting into her partner's story of growing up in an orphanage in Canada. When it was her turn to talk, Jean enjoyed telling her partner, Max, how she'd always felt inferior to her older brother and of the violent arguments they'd had.

When the talking/listening part of the exercise ended, the facilitator added two additional tasks. First each partner got a minute to tell his or her good points. This was hard; Jean kept wanting to tell Max what was wrong with her. Finally, each had a minute to tell what each liked about the other person.

Although everyone in the room found certain parts of the exercise difficult, the general feeling was positive. Almost all participants said they felt as if they'd made a friend.

Kathie, a black woman, put it this way: "My partner here who is white told me she liked my nonthreatening attitude. If I hadn't gotten to know her first, I might have taken that as a put-down. We blacks are supposed to be hostile, you know." Kathie turned to her new friend and grinned. "But because I'd gotten to know her first, I believed she meant the statement as a compliment, and I took it that way."

Chené explained that one thing most people have in common is the tendency to dislike saying nice things about themselves. "It doesn't feel right to us. Most of us have been more put down than built up; therefore, we feel more comfortable saying what's wrong with ourselves than what's right."

The facilitator went on to explain that although the talking/listening exercise is contrived and structured, it illustrates the importance of taking time to listen. "This is the way human beings should always relate."

Jean still wasn't sure what the exercise had to do with cross-cultural conflict resolution. "In our listening," said Chené, "we structured equality. Someone has to take responsibility for guaranteeing respect. We modeled a mutual relationship. Letting people be who they are builds trust. By listening we create respect."

"More," said someone in the audience, "more!"

Chené nodded. "If I respect what you tell me, I discover what we have in common. If we start by accepting our differences, we discover our common humanity."

Jean nodded. That made sense. She thought back to all the times her parents had ordered her to do this or that and how often she had conveniently "forgotten."

"By letting people be themselves," Chené went on, "we create safety in the relationship. We say, 'It's okay to be who you are. Next comes self-esteem: The person feels good about herself. And finally, we *tell* her she's good." Chené repeated his message: "When you eliminate choice, you create conflict. It happens all the time in families—adults impose themselves, and the children rebel."

Jean thought about home. Could she persuade her parents to let her become an equal partner in negotiating solutions to some of their disagreements? An exciting idea, thought Jean. Definitely worth a try.

Chené went on. "Dominant/subordinate relationships. That's where the trouble starts. In fact, that's the principle of white racism. The relationship between the cultures becomes a one-way street that is coercive and dysfunctional. The result is anger passed down from one generation to the next. Those in the majority, those who have the power, expect everyone else to be exactly like them; many people are intolerant of differentness. 'Become like me,' they say, 'and then we can get along.' The anger has to come out in some way. When we're put in competition with others, the rage we've pushed deep inside ourselves erupts—sometimes in very strange and harmful ways. Anger at the Rodney King verdict was one example. Anything can be a trigger. The wrong verdict, for example."

Chené asked the members of the group to think of a time someone had stereotyped them. Jean raised her hand. "My science teacher, Mr. Higgins, did. Once because someone else interrupted him, Mr. Higgins called *me* a dumb blonde."

"Good example," said Chené. "Now, if you meet me, and I look a lot like Mr. Higgins, are you going to like me?"

Jean shook her head.

"Another trigger for anger," Chené said.

"But what can we do about it?" Jean asked. "How can we change our homes plus our schools and communities?"

Chené rubbed his chin. "One of the things we have to do is acknowledge our differences and go on from there. We're stuck in denial if we say there is no difference or we don't have any bias."

Kathie's partner stood up and gestured at Kathie. "You mean as in, 'Oh, I didn't notice you were black?'"

People in the audience laughed along with Chené. "Exactly," he said. "Let's face it, we're stuck with each other. No one is going back wherever it was he or she came from. We have to start by taking the time to talk and to listen, to validate each other's equality."

A man in the middle of the room stood up. "It looks as if Rodney King had the right idea—about people getting along, I mean."

"That's about it," said Chené. "We tend to get locked in our rigid roles. But when trust breaks down over time, we have to start over. We need healing. To bring about healing, each of us must be willing to change."

*   *   *

At the end of the conference, Jean hated to leave. She went back to her school with a desire to change herself and to change others. But do most young people in today's society *want* change? As mentioned earlier, some students feel helpless, but others speak of possible understanding and hope. The following sample of responses suggests that they do want change.

- "Just because a person is different from you in some way doesn't mean he or she isn't as good as you."
- "I wish I could express how I feel about the situation of mixing people. People need to take the view of little children. We are all equal in the nursery and at the cemetery."
- "I believe everyone should be treated alike. Don't we all bleed when we're cut? Don't we all hurt when we get sick? Don't we all eat when we get hungry? There isn't that much difference in people. It shouldn't matter if a person is black or white, Spanish or Indian, pink or blue, ugly or pretty. I don't understand why there is so much bias in this world."
- "I wish bias incidents wouldn't happen, but I'm afraid they will for a long time to come. I don't know how people can stand to treat others in such ways. Certain people can't seem to live with themselves, so they take their hurts out on others they think are different."
- "I believe people can be cruel. I know almost everyone out there has been a victim and has felt hurt, even if they didn't do anything to anybody. I know I have. It hurts on both ends. We need to resolve this problem."

WHAT CAN WE DO?

Become Culturally Competent

If young people sincerely want to end bias incidents, the first step is to become culturally competent. That means not only showing respect for those of different cultures but showing respect for those who are different in any way.

The *Colorado Alumnus* (Fall 1992) features Lerita Coleman, a black associate professor of psychology at the University of Colorado. Coleman has been studying individual differences for a decade. She holds that all cultures tend to stigmatize those who are different. Therefore, as noted before, almost everyone has at one time or another felt stigmatized. Some people are able to transcend the stigma; they "come to understand that they are not this bad thing that others respond negatively to, that fundamental similarities outweigh differences."

Native American Terry Cross (first mentioned in Chapter 1) gives this advice. Cultural competence includes attitudes, skills, policies, and structures that help us function in cross-cultural situations. Unless you live on Mars, you are likely to encounter cross-cultural situations in everyday life. Even if you live in a small town with little racial or ethnic diversity, you at least relate to people older than you, as well as those of the opposite sex. Chances are that at some time in your life you will move to another part of the country or travel outside the country. At such times you may find Cross's tips helpful.

The first part of becoming culturally competent is recognizing that differences exist. We are not all the same; we are not even remotely the same. If John Jones says, "I'm color-blind; everyone's really the same," John is slightly off-base. While we can admire his goal of racial and ethnic harmony, John is ignoring or playing down the richness of cultural strengths and traditions.

Terry Cross tells of a Native-American boy, Dexter, age thirteen. For years Dexter attended the reservation school, where all his classmates were of the same ethnicity. Dexter learned, however, that some of the people he met in town had a different cultural history. He accepted these differences. Of course I'm different, Dexter thought. I like my dark hair and tan skin. Then Dexter became aware of his own cultural values. At the reservation school, most students shared the things they owned. If Dexter needed a pencil, he borrowed one from his neighbor. If his neighbor needed an eraser, Dexter expected to share his. But when Dexter moved to the city school and borrowed someone's pencil, the other kids accused him of stealing. Clearly, Dexter had to learn new values to live successfully in a multicultural world.

Finally, someone like Dexter has to understand that he is living in two worlds. He has to learn to enjoy the best of both worlds. Wouldn't it be nice if other people got to know him and tried to understand what he is going through?

Become an Activist

The second big step is to become an activist. We discussed activism in Chapter 2. To become an activist we need to stop talking and *do* something. Rosa Parks was a person who made a difference. This young woman's refusal to give up her bus seat helped spark the civil rights movement. Parks understood that she was a person of worth and took action to prove it.

In their book *Taking a Stand Against Racism and Racial Discrimination*, Patricia and Frederick McKissack suggest that anyone can become an activist. One of the most important things anyone can do is to vote. Statistics show that less than half of potential voters eighteen to twenty-four even bother to *register*. Less than 25 percent actually vote. What can *you* do? Find a political candidate you can support, someone who states clearly his or her positions against racism and discrimination; then vote for that person. If you're not old enough to vote, volunteer to help with a campaign. It's fun and educational.

Another activist move is to organize something. Bobbi Miller, seventeen, helped her mother organize a multi-ethnic community festival with ethnic foods, dances, and crafts. Proceeds from the fair helped the parents of needy youngsters pay for after-school enrichment programs. The event was so popular that it became an annual affair. Will Jones, sixteen, and his dad organized a graffiti-removing, alley-cleaning potluck in their interracial neighborhood. Working together brought about friendships among neighbors who had never before even spoken to each other.

Other actions include keeping a record of your thoughts about and actions toward those who are different from you in some way. How do your thoughts and actions contribute to stereotyping, scapegoating, and racism? What about your favorite TV shows? Do they perpetuate racism? Have you ever seen or read literature from hate groups? Be aware that these groups often target teenagers to spread their messages of hate.

Find out more about your own cultural heritage. Did one of your grandparents arrive as an immigrant on Ellis Island? Can you find out the details? Chances are your grandparents would love to share their stories with you.

In addition to your usual friends, find someone "different" to relate to. If you can't find someone in your town, get a pen pal in another country. Learn something about his or her cultural heritage or religion.

Susan, fifteen

"In middle school, black students and white students each made up approximately half the school. Neither group knew what to expect of the other. I tried to be friendly to everyone. After a few weeks when students got to know each other, some people became friends with those of different races. The wall that had separated people came tumbling down. I realized that color doesn't really matter; a person's core is the same—no matter what."

A next step in activism is not to put up with prejudice. Let your acquaintances know that racism and bigotry are not okay. If someone makes a racial remark, let the speaker know your feelings. Getting involved may mean joining a protest movement against discrimination. Lawful protests include writing letters to newspapers and congresspersons, circulating petitions, or carrying signs in a peaceful demonstration.

Carl, twenty-one

Carl was a college junior when he heard that his neighbor, an employee of the fair housing bureau, needed volunteers for a project to discover whether or not minorities were being discriminated against. Every Sunday afternoon for several months, Carl, who is white, went apartment-hunting with a partner, Denise, who is black. The two pretended to be married. Before their arrival at a specific rental property, a white couple had preceded them. Carl and Denise found much less acceptance than the all-white couple. The data collected in the study gave the bureau ammunition as they pressed for stronger fair-housing laws.

Other things you can do are to attend cultural festivities and gatherings organized by minority members of your community, or visit a display of Native-American crafts or an exhibit about black history.

Finally, try this role-modeling exercise: (1) Name five personal heroes or heroines. (2) Why and how did these persons influence you? (3) Are these role models doing what you might like to be doing twenty or thirty years from now? (4) Are these people from the same or different ethnic background as yours? (5) Would you enjoy watching TV or reading books and magazines if you rarely saw a person of your racial/ethnic group portrayed?

HOPEFUL SIGNS

Anthropologist Margaret Mead said: "Never doubt that a small group of thoughtful and committed citizens can change the world; indeed, it's the only thing that ever has." For those who hope for a bias-free society and more respect for members of minority groups, are there any hopeful signs? Here are some examples. Do you know of others?

- High school students in a Western state have organized themselves into a small but growing movement called ERP (Eliminate Racial Prejudice). The senior class distributed red buttons with the ERP initials to those willing to sign a pledge that they would work to eliminate racial prejudice and would not engage in violent behavior.

- The percentage of blacks with annual household incomes of $50,000 or more grew by 182 percent between 1970 and 1989, almost double the increase among whites at that level. (In spite of this encouraging news, Charles King of the Urban Crisis Center points out that such statistics can blind white Americans to more depressing news: At least a third of all blacks still live below the poverty level; at least a third of all black families are headed by single women.)

- Former Cleveland Brown football star Jim Brown has been turning gang members around with his rehabilitation business, Amer-I-Can (*USA Weekend*, July 31-August 2, 1992). Brown's three-year-old program teaches self-esteem, how to deal with families and emotions, how to communicate, how to solve problems, and how to look for a job. His only requirement is that participants want to improve their lives. So far more than 7,500 prison inmates and hundreds of gang members have graduated from the program, which gives African-Americans the tools for survival.

- In Colorado Springs, the same city in which a soldier died from repeated kicks to the head, a black Army sergeant saved a nine-year-old white boy from drowning in a rain-swollen drainage ditch. Although the hero couldn't swim, he said he would have done the same for anyone.

- In the summer of 1992, a nine-year-old Anglo boy on an outing with his day-care group saved a black toddler from drowning at a popular reservoir.

- A Chicano artist, Joaquin Mares, painted a bright acrylic mural of symbols representing Mexican tradition and Chicano power at a Cinco de Mayo celebration. Mares said his mural gives people of other cultures a chance to see a piece of Mexican history. Another Chicano artist, Andy Mendoza, agreed. "If we know a little about each other, we are less likely to discriminate against one another."
- More black-owned businesses are selling items reflecting the culture and heritage of African-Americans. Some, such as Cross Colours Fashions, target a multicultural market. The number of exhibitors at the Black Expo USA 1992 trade show in New York City doubled from 1989 levels. "Ethnic marketing" has increased since the 1990 census showed that people of African, Hispanic, Native-American, and Asian heritage make up about one-fourth of the U.S. population.
- A piece of good news from the 1990 census is that women and minorities have moved into the American workplace in occupations denied to them only a decade ago. The *Miami Herald* did a computer analysis that showed significant progress for women. In 1960 two of three American workers were white males; in 1990 white males made up 45 percent of the workforce.
- Native Americans believe their long holocaust may be ending. In the Year of the American Indian (1992), five hundred years after Christopher Columbus, Native Americans said with pride, "We're still here." For the first time since Columbus, Indian lands, power, and pride are growing.
- Native Americans have also begun to make their mark in the business world. Don Kellin, a Caddo

Indian from Oklahoma, owns Caddo Design, Inc., a company specializing in the design and installation of modular office systems. Kellin says, "We want our people to become self-sufficient in the American society by improving education, increasing our business skills, by working closely with non-Indian businesses, associations, agencies, and individuals that have an interest in seeing us succeed."

- Elizabeth Schneider of Brooklyn Law School says that in the past twenty years women's groups have managed to persuade others that domestic violence is an aspect of gender discrimination. Domestic violence relates to other issues such as economic discrimination, sex segregation in the job market, discrimination against women in the family, rape, and other forms of violence. Legislation recently introduced in Congress would define violence against women as a hate crime and, therefore, a violation of the civil rights of women.

- U.S. Representative Patricia Schroeder of Colorado recently introduced two bills designed to prevent sexual harassment in the military and to provide assistance to victims of sexual violence in the armed forces.

- The Anti-Defamation League in Colorado sponsored a family-oriented Bike Against Bigotry in the summer of 1992. For further information, write to the Anti-Defamation League of B'Nai B'rith, 832 United Nations Plaza, New York, NY, 10017.

- The Council on Interracial Books for Children (CIBC) grew out of a belief that children "must be raised in a bias-free environment if they are to develop a positive self-identity and openness to people of other backgrounds and beliefs." Established in 1965, the CIBC makes linkages between racism and other kinds of bias—sexism, ageism, militarism, and homophobia. For further information about this organization, write to Council on Interracial Books for Children, 1841 Broadway, New York, NY 10023-7648.

- Bookstore owner Sue Lubeck says the world is getting smaller. Recently she has noticed that publishers are bringing out more and more ethnic and multicultural books.

- After the Los Angeles riots of 1992, songwriters composed healing songs. Riot victims received the proceeds of some of these songs. Singer and song-writer Stevie Wonder believes that love is the key. Love can conquer all evil, he suggests. "It's there inside you, if you'll only listen."

- The nation's forty-three million disabled citizens should find doors opening with the implementation of the Americans with Disabilities Act. The law, called a "declaration of independence" for the disabled, requires that businesses be made acces-sible by the end of January 1992. Other clauses of the act will take effect in the near future.

- Increasingly, people are realizing that working together is the way to solve problems. One example is the Intercultural Leadership Program. In April 1991, Santa Fe Community College received a four-year grant from the W.K. Kellogg Foundation to lead the way toward improving community problem-solving. For further information about this program, write or call the Intercultural Community Leadership Project, Santa Fe Community College, P.O. Box 4187, Santa Fe, NM 87502-4187, (505) 471-8200.

An Attitude of Healing

Remember the incident in Chapter 1 in which four assailants sprayed two black youngsters with shoe polish? Afterward the children's mother, Nellie Wilson, modeled an attitude of healing: "I try to tell my kids not everybody who is white is bad. They just met some sour apples, some bad people. At least the people taking care of them are white," she added, referring to the police detectives. "Maybe that will have a good influence on them." When her son expressed doubts about the survival of his friendships with whites, she replied, "If they're your friends, then give them the benefit of the doubt."

At the same time, New York officials met to discuss what actions to take to stop those who would spread hate. Mayor David Dinkins, the first black mayor of New York City, called on residents "to begin a new movement based on nonviolence." He said that the solutions to violence lie not with the police but with better role models at home, in the building of stronger families.

Let's All Get Along

None of us can solve the problems of prejudice and bias incidents singlehandedly, but by working together we can make progress. Xernona Clayton, an Atlanta civic leader for more than two generations, says: "Prejudice means the individual fails to grow, fails to be enlarged by encounters and experiences and exchanges with others, fails to learn and appreciate the diversity of humankind. What person who aspires to be intelligent and modern and spiritually alive could want to practice discrimination and segregation? No fairminded person does."

Can't we all get along?

Appendix

BIAS-FIGHTING ORGANIZATIONS

American Civil Liberties Union (ACLU)
132 West 43rd Street
New York, NY 10036

Anti-Defamation League of B'Nai B'rith
832 United Nations Plaza
New York, NY 10017

Asian American Legal Defense and Education Fund
99 Hudson Street
New York, NY 10013

Asian Immigrant Women Advocates
310 8th Street
Oakland, CA 94607

Japanese American Citizens League
1730 Rhode Island Avenue NW
Washington, DC 20036

Klanwatch
P.O. Box 548
Montgomery AL 36195

Martin Luther King Center for Nonviolent Social Change
449 Auburn Avenue NE
Atlanta, GA 30312

National Association for the Advancement of Colored People
(NAACP)

4805 Mt. Hope Drive
Baltimore, MD 21215

National Congress of American Indians
900 Pennsylvania Avenue SE
Washington, DC 20003

National Institute Against Prejudice and Violence
31 South Greene Street
Baltimore, MD 21201

National Organization for Women
1000 16th Street NW
Washington, DC 20036

National Urban League
500 East 62nd Street
New York, NY 10021

Native American Rights Fund
1506 Broadway
Boulder, CO 80302

People United to Save Humanity (Operation PUSH)
930 East 50th Street
Chicago, IL 60615

U.S. Department of Justice Community Relations Service
5550 Friendship Boulevard
Chevy Chase, MD 20815

For Further Reading

Allport, Gordon. *The Nature of Prejudice*. New York: Addison-Wesley Publishing Company, Inc., 1958.

Anti-Defamation League of B'nai B'rith, et al. *A World of Difference*. Denver, 1990.

Bard, Morton, and Sangrey, Dawn. *The Crime Victim's Book*. New York: Basic Books, Inc., 1979.

Berry, Joy. *Every Kid's Guide to Overcoming Prejudice and Discrimination*. Chicago: Children's Press, 1987.

Bramson, Robert. *Coping with Difficult People*. Garden City, NY: Anchor Press/Doubleday, 1981.

Clayton, Xernona, with Gulliver, Hal. *I've Been Marching All the Time*. Atlanta: Longstreet Press, 1991.

Derman-Sparks, Louise, and the A.B.C. Task Force. *Anti-Bias Curriculum*. Washington, DC: National Association for the Education of Young Children, 1991.

Edwards, Audrey, and Polite, Craig. *Children of the Dream: The Psychology of Black Success*. New York: Doubleday, 1992.

Edwards, Gabrielle I. *Coping with Discrimination*. New York: Rosen Publishing, 1992.

Fersh, Seymour, ed. *Learning About Peoples and Cultures*. Evanston, IL: McDougal, Littell & Company, 1989.

Ford Foundation Women's Program Forum. *Violence Against Women: Addressing a Global Program*. New York: Ford Foundation, 1992.

Flynn, Kevin, and Gerhardt, Gary. *The Silent Brotherhood*. New York: Penguin Books, 1989.

Gabelko, Nina, and Michaelis, John. *Reducing Adolescent Prejudice*. New York: Teachers College Press, 1981.

Gibbs, Jewelle, and Huagn, Larke and Associates. *Children of Color: Psychological Interventions with Minority Youth*. San Francisco: Jossey-Bass, Inc., 1989.

Grosshandler, Janet. *Coping with Verbal Abuse*. New York: Rosen Publishing, 1989.

Hacker, Andrew. *Two Nations*. New York: Charles Scribner's Sons, 1992.

Heldman, Mary Lynne. *When Words Hurt: How to Keep Criticism from Undermining Your Self-Esteem*. New York: Ballantine Books, 1988.

Helmreich, William. *The Things They Say Behind Your Back*. New Brunswick, NJ: Transactions Books, 1984.

Hopson, Darlene and Derek. *Different and Wonderful: Raising Black Children in a Race-Conscious Society*. New York: Prentice-Hall Press, 1990.

Jackson, Edward. *Black Education in Contemporary America*. Bristol, IN: Wyndam Hall Press, 1983.

Katz, Judith. *White Awareness: Handbook for Anti-Racism Training*. Norman: University of Oklahoma Press, 1989.

Kochman, Thomas. *Black and White: Styles in Conflict*. Chicago: University of Chicago Press, 1983.

Kovel, Joel. *White Racism*. New York: Columbia University Press, 1984.

Kunjufu, Jawanza. *To Be Popular or Smart: The Black Peer Group*. Chicago: African American Images, 1988.

———. *Countering the Conspiracy to Destroy Black Boys*, Vols. I, II, and III. Chicago: Afro-Am Publishing Co., 1984, 1986, 1988.

Lewis, Bernard. *Semites and Anti-Semites*. New York: W.W. Norton & Company, 1986.

Lucas, Eileen. *Peace on the Playground: Nonviolent Ways of Problem-Solving*. New York: Franklin Watts, 1991.

Loeb, Robert. *The Sins of Bias*. New York: M. Evans and Company, 1970.

McKissack, Patricia and Frederick. *Taking a Stand Against Racism and Racial Discrimination*. New York: Franklin Watts, 1990.

Milner, David. *Children and Race*. London: Sage Publications, Inc., 1983.

Molebatsi, Caesar, with Virtue, David. *A Flame for Justice*. Oxford: Lion Publishing, 1991.

National School Safety Center. *Gangs in Schools: Breaking Up Is Hard to Do*. Malibu, CA: Pepperdine University Press, 1991.

Parks, Rosa, with Haskins, Jim. *Rosa Parks: My Story*. New York: Dial Books, 1992.

Pickens, Judy. *Without Bias: A Guidebook for Nondiscriminatory Communication*. New York: Wiley, 1982.

Rosenberg, Maxine. *Living in Two Worlds*. New York: Lothrop, Lee & Shepard Books, 1986.

Segal, Julius. *Winning Life's Toughest Battles*. New York: McGraw-Hill Book Company, 1986.

Smith, Errol. *37 Things Every Black Man Needs to Know*. Valencia, CA: St. Clair Rene Publishing, 1991.

Smith, Sandra Lee. *Coping with Cross-Cultural and Interracial Relationships*. New York: Rosen Publishing, 1990.

Sojourners Magazine Editors. *America's Original Sin: A Study of White Racism*. Washington, DC: Sojourners, 1988.

Steele, Shelby. *The Content of Our Character: A New Vision of Race in America*. New York: HarperPerennial, 1991.

Tucker, Richard. *The Dragon and the Cross: The Rise and Fall of the Ku Klux Klan in Middle America*. Hamden, CT: Archon Books, 1991.

Ury, William. *Getting Past No: Negotiating with Difficult People*. New York: Bantam Books, 1991.

Weeks, Dudley. *The Eight Essential Steps to Conflict Resolution*. Los Angeles: Jeremy P. Tarcher, Inc., 1992.

Webster-Doyle, Terrence. *Why Is Everybody Always Picking On Me?* Middlebury, VT: Atrium Publications, 1991.

Index

A

abuse, physical, 60–61, 72, 78–82
acquaintance rape, 58–60
activism, 41, 100, 134–137
African-Americans, 4–5, 8, 9, 17, 49–50, 65, 66, 68, 95, 102, 123, 139; *see also* blacks
age
  bias, 3, 46, 68–69, 110–111
  stereotyping, 30
Albanian Boys, 66–67
alcohol, 58, 62
Allport, Gordon, 6, 21, 28, 34, 36–37, 64, 72–73
Anderson, Elijah, 43
anger, using healthy, 99–102
Anglos, 13, 14–15, 24–25, 74, 79, 84, 95, 102, 105, 123–124; *see also* whites
Anti-Bias Curriculum, 40–41
Anti-Defamation League, 140
anti-Semitism, 2, 83
anxiety, of victim, 91
Asian-Americans, 4, 6, 9, 11, 66, 139
assertiveness, 102–103
avoidance, as bias, 72, 74

B

Bard, Morton, 113–114
Bennett, Maisha, 42–43
bias
  crimes, 15
  defined, 1–23
  defusing, 81–82, 110–112
  handling, 86–126
  kinds of, 72–85
  origins of, 24–45
  sources of, 46–71
  turf, 65–68
bigotry, 9, 13–15
  opposing, 136–137
blacks, 4–5, 8, 9, 11, 15–16, 25, 26, 32–33, 40, 42–43, 46–47, 49, 73, 74, 75–76, 91, 93, 95, 109–110; *see also* African-Americans
  life threats to, 17–18, 19
  self-esteem of, 22
Brown, Jim, 138
Brown, Lee P., 59–60
Burke, James Lee, 7

C

Campbell, Phil, 84–85
Carosello, Cindy, 59
Charleston, Steve, 27

Children of Color, 4–5, 17
Children of the Dream, 63
Civil Rights, U.S. Commission
    on, 5, 32
Clayton, Xernona, 142–143
Coady, Elizabeth, 116
Coleman, Lerita, 133
college, bias in, 50–51
communication, in coping with
    bias, 104–106
compassion, 108–109
competence, cultural, 133–134
conflict resolution, 128–132
conscience, clear, 107–108
contraception, 61
control, taking, 106–107
conviction, in bias incidents,
    107
Council on Interracial Books for
    Children, 140–141
*Countering the Threat to
    Destroy Black Boys*, 17–18
Cross, Terry, 14–15, 133–134

D
date rape, 58–60
Derman-Sparks, Louise, 40–41
Dinkins, David, 84–85, 142
discrimination, 12–13, 72,
    76–78
diversity, cultural, 4–5, 24–25,
    107, 118, 127–132
Doyle, Daniel, 62–63

E
Edwards, Audrey, 63
extermination, 72, 82–85

F
fanaticism, 9
fear, as cause of prejudice,
    43–44
females
    life threats to, 17
    stereotyping of, 29–30, 77
    fighting back, 2, 92, 94–95
    fight, refusal to, 109–110

G
Gabelko, Nina, 13
Gallo, Nic, 122–123
gangs, 65–67, 95
Gaskin, Pearl, 15
gays. *see* homosexuals
gender bias, 5
generalizations, 20–21, 39
Getting Past No, 87–91
Gibbs, Jewelle, 17
Gordon, Gilbert, 18
Guernsey, Bruce, 62
Guillaume, Robert, 99
guilt, feelings of, 96–97, 107

H
Handgun Control, 84
Harrington, Maureen, 61
Harrison, Greg, 56
hate crimes, 6–9, 43, 108
hatred, ethnic, 9
Hendricks, Eve, 56–57
Hill, Anita, 55
Hispanics, 4–5, 9, 11, 15, 25,
    35, 40, 41–42, 50, 62, 66,
    76, 77, 84, 95, 111, 139
Hitler, Adolf, 8, 52–53, 73, 83,
    92
Holocaust, 25, 73, 82–83

homosexuals, 61–63
  hate crimes against, 6–7, 83
  stereotyping of, 30
Hopson, Darlene and Derek,
  22, 106
housing, segregation in, 51–52
humor, use of, 111–112

I
identity, personal, 21–22, 118
"I" messages, 101, 105
in-groups, 35–37, 38
Irons, Edward, 65

J
Jews, 8, 9, 14, 20, 25, 28–29,
  32, 39–40, 50, 52–53, 54,
  74, 76, 82–83, 91–92
judgments, preconceived, 9, 21

K
karate, 109
Kellin, Don, 139–140
King, Charles, 12
King, Rodney, 4, 9, 43, 131
Klanwatch, 6
Korean-Americans, 49–50
Ku Klux Klan, 6–7, 52–53, 81
Kunjufu, Jawanza, 17, 106

L
labeling, 39–42
Lahti, Christine, 55–56
Lee, Spike, 64
lesbianism, 3, 61–62
Levinson, Arlene, 65
life, threats to, 17–18, 82–85
listener, being a good, 119–122

loyalty, minority group, 92–95
Lubeck, Sue, 141

M
Making Friends, 104
Mares, Joaquin, 139
Massey, Douglas, 19
McKissack, Patricia and
  Frederick, 134–135
Mead, Margaret, 137
Meeks, Catherine, 12
Mendoza, Andy, 139
Michaelis, John, 13
military, harassment in, 56
Miller, George, 4–5
Moral Majority, 7
myths and facts
  about gangs, 65–66
  about prejudice, 15–18
  about rape, 58–59

N
National Gay and Lesbian Task
  Force, 7, 61
Native Americans, 4–5, 14–15,
  25, 27, 102, 133–134, 139
Nature of Prejudice, The, 6
neighborhoods, bias in, 51–52
neo-Nazis, 6, 8, 52–53
nonviolent skills, 109–113
Novello, Antonia, 58, 60

O
Olivas, Jorge and Genaro,
  83–84
onlooker, in bias incidents,
  117–122
out-groups, 37–38

P
parents, as source of prejudice,
    34, 60
Perot, Ross, 44–45
Polite, Craig, 63
posttraumatic stress disorder,
    125
prejudice, 9–10, 12, 14–15, 44
    against disabled, 69–71, 112
    biracial, 77, 79–80, 86–91,
        111, 117, 123–124
    ethnic, 48, 49–53, 75, 80, 96,
        107–109, 114–115,
        116–117
    gender, 4, 28–29, 46, 54–63,
        77
    against homosexuals, 3, 6–7,
        30, 61–63, 83
    racial, 1, 4–5, 28–29, 33–34,
        46–47
    religious, 2, 4–5, 13–14, 20,
        25, 39, 46, 53–54
    against sexual orientation,
        4–5, 30, 46
    social/economic class, 4–5,
        19–20, 30, 42–43, 46,
        63–65, 74

R
racial tension, 6–7
Race . . . the American
    Obsession, 18
racism, 9, 12–13, 14–15, 43
    economic, 63–64
    opposing, 136–137
    as white problem, 24–25, 27
rape, date and acquaintance,
    58–60

recovery, from bias incident,
    113–117
Reducing Adolescent Prejudice,
    13
rejection, as bias, 72, 75–76
relationship, violent, 60, 61
Reproductive Health, 61
Rivera, Julio, 62–63, 65
role playing, 112–113
Roy, Joseph T., 6

S
Sangrey, Dawn, 113–114
scapegoating, 28–33, 44,
    52–53, 65
Schmidtke, Layne, 68
Schneider, Elizabeth, 140
school
    ethnic bias in, 114–115
    sexual harassment in, 56–57,
        77–78
    turf bias in, 67–68
    violence in, 84
Schroeder, Patricia, 140
Segal, Julius, 104–109
self-esteem, 21–22, 81,
    103–104, 118
self-hate, 95
self-help groups, 125–126
sexism, 2, 55
sexual harassment, 55–58
skinheads, 5, 8, 15, 39
Smith, Errol, 97
status
    desire for, 34–35
    killing for, 42–43, 64–65
stereotyping, 10–11, 14–15,
    28–31, 44
stoners, 66, 67

stress, handling, 122–125
Sullivan, Louis, 16

T
talk, biased, 72–73
Terkel, Studs, 18–19
Thatcher, Margaret, 119
Thomas, Cal, 83
Thomas, Clarence, 55
Tune In to Your Rights, 58

U
Ury, William, 87–91

V
values, democratic, 44, 52–53
victims of bias, 91–92, 104
violence
    in bias incidents, 72, 83–85
    gang, 65–66
    against homosuxuals, 61–63,
        65
    against women, 60

W
Wallis, Jim, 27, 63–64
Waters, Maxine, 50
Webster-Doyle, Terrence, 109
whites; *see also* Anglos
    attacks on, 59
    as minority, 38–39
    as powerful, 12–13, 27
    prejudice against, 8, 15–16,
        18–19, 35, 37, 38, 47–48,
        73, 79, 80
    stereotyping, 25–26
Whye, Chet, 63
*Why Is Everybody Always
    Picking on Me?*, 109
Wiesel, Elie, 9, 119
*Winning Life's Toughest
    Battles*, 104–109
women
    sisterhood of, 94–95
    violence against, 60–61
Wonder, Stevie, 141
world problem, bias as 52–53